Contents

BUREAUCRAZY GETS CRAZIER

IAS Unmasked

Other Books and Creative Works by (the author)

In English

As Oasis of Solitude (Writers' Workshop, Calcutta, 1973)	Poetry
Look Closely at Om (Writers' Workshop, Calcutta, 1976)	Poetry
China: The Training System (FAO, 1979)	Monograph
The Science of Spirituality (D.K. Publishers, Delhi, 1983)	Spirituality
Kusha Grass (Siddhartha Publications, Chandigarh, 1985)	Poetry
The Sandalwood Door (Konark Publications, Delhi, 1985)	Poetry
Life is a Squirrel (Konark Publications, Delhi, 1994)	Poetry
Kashmir: Its Life and People (Edited, APH Publications, Delhi)	Sociology
Kashmir Shaivism (Sai International Centre, Delhi, 2001)	Philosophy

In Hindi

Kehna Aasaan Hai (Parag Prakashan, Delhi, 1982)	Poetry
Aasamaan Nahin Girte (Parag Prakashan, Delhi 1984)	Novel
Ikshwaku Se (Disha Prakashan, 1985)	Poetry

Snowman (Abhiyan Prakashan, 1986)	Short Stories
Charhte Panni se Baakhabar (Kitab Ghar, 1996)	Poetry
Dal Thhandi Ho Rahi Hai (Sarrika, 1986)	Play
Panditji Aa Gaye (Saarika, 1986)	Play
Prem Vibhag (Saarika, 1986)	Play
Zindabad Murdabad (Saarika, 1986)	Play
Niyam Nahin Hai (Saarika, 1986)	Play

Television

Zindabad Murdabad (Jalandhar Doordarshan Kendra, 1987)	Teleplay
Kehna Aasaan Hai (Kashir TV Channel, 1999)	13-episode TV Serial

BUREAUCRAZY GETS CRAZIER

IAS Unmasked

M.K. KAW

Konark Publishers Pvt Ltd
New Delhi

Konark Publishers Pvt. Ltd
206, First Floor,
Peacock Lane, Shahpur Jat,
New Delhi-110 049.
Phone: +91-11-4105 5065
e-mail: india@konarkpublishers.com; us@konarkpublishers.com
Website: www.konarkpublishers.com

Thirteenth Impression 2023

Cataloging in Publication Data--DK
Courtesy: D.K. Agencies (P) Ltd. <docinfo@dkagencies.com>

Kaw, M. K., 1941-
Bureaucrazy gets crazier : IAS unmasked / M.K. Kaw.
p. cm.
ISBN 9789322008086

1. Humorous stories, Indic (English). I. Title.

DDC 823.92 23

Typeset and Design by: SPB Enterprises Pvt. Ltd., www.spbenterprises.net.in

Printed and bound at Saurabh Printers Pvt. Ltd.

To the most important women in my life—

Somawati (mother)

Raj (wife)

Asha (sister)

Iti (daughter)

Urvashi (daughter-in-law)

Monaal (grand daughter)

PART FOUR
GOING LIKE A BOMB

PART FIVE
A RUM GO

PART SIX
GOING THROUGH THE STARTOSPHERE

Why there is a sequel

If a book makes you laugh, is that not enough? Do we need to delve into the reason why there is a sequel?

P.G. Wodehouse wrote so many books on Jeeves that he felt obliged to explain away the phenomenon. He found that writing a Jeeves book was like the urge to smoke. He would often resolve not to write another, but the urge became unbearable. The most difficult was the period just following breakfast.

The problem is that bureaucrazy is becoming crazier by the minute. Two young Joshis break all records by filching away all of

Rs 400 crores in the first fifteen years of service. One cannot easily stomach the theory that a poor diminutive Raja could singlehandedly have swallowed and digested the unpronouncable sum of a hundred and seventy five thousand crores of 2G kickbacks. But the CAG says so and the CAG is an honourable man.

The Government's response is unprecedented in its hamhandedness and foolishness. In 1967 when I was a junior Magistrate there was a procession by naga sadhus, who threatened to gate-crash into the Parliament house. The Deputy Commissioner had left the scene of action as soon as he felt it turning hot. I bleated, "What are the orders, Sir?" He hurried past impatiently. "I have imposed Section 144. Go and enforce it. I am rushing to headquarters to fetch additional police contingents."

This yielded the precious nugget of wisdom, which I expressed as an aphorism thus: "Wisdom lies in presence of mind and absence of body."

Today, the Government adopts 21st century techniques to counter the Babas. First, they are given a royal reception, hoping that they would fall for it and call off the fast unto death or whatever. When this fails, the police launch a midnight operation and lathi-charge sleeping women and children. The little-known Baba is transformed into a national figure. Now the Government appoints a drafting committee with five ministers and five members of Team Anna. This results in a farce in five acts and makes a laughing stock of the Government.

None of us retired bureaucrats can believe that the screenplay for this incredible farce has been penned by our successors in the Service.

In our times, everyone knew that black money was stashed away in foreign bank accounts in Switzerland and other tax havens. But we had a reasonable basis for inaction. The authorities refused to divulge the names and addresses of the accountholders. Today, the tables have been turned. The authorities are prepared to divulge the details if we approach them via their courts in the proper way. And we have and they have. But have we published the names for general information of the public? You can bet your trouser buttons we have not!!!

For some time, the Government carried on by the sheer weight of the grey-bearded sardar in the light blue turban who mumbled absentmindedly into his moustache and drove a Maruti 800 car. But the ubiquitous presence of the black-bearded Sardar in the light blue turban who did not mumble into his moustache spoilt the entire impression.

When we played chess in those days, the fundamental danger one had to watch out for was the safety of the king. On no account was his safety to be compromised. The entire army might be intact; just the missing king was enough to lose the game. Today the opposition's opening gambit is a virulent attack on the king. He is under check all the time. If you fail to concentrate even for a nano second, it is checkmate and the king is gone.

And when the king is gone, the game is up!

Thus far the justification for a sequel. But is this really a sequel? A sequel is a follow-up of a theme already explored, with the same characters facing different situations. So if it were a sequel, I would call it Bureaucrazy 2 or Bureaucrazy II. This really is Bureaucrazy Revised, Updated and Enlarged.

Why there is a sequel

I can never forget an incident that took place on board the Guwahati-Delhi flight, soon after Bureaucrazy was first published in 1993. I was reading a book. Happening to glance at my co-passengers, I was flabbergasted to see an unusual sight: a middle-aged smartly-dressed gentleman smiling all to himself. Smiling was hardly the act; he was chortling silently, trying to contain an inner merriment and failing to. After some time, I just could not resist finding out the cause.

I got up as if to visit the loo and was intrigued to see that a book was the cause of this gaiety and now I said to myself, I have positively, definitely to see what book has this power. You cannot imagine how humble I felt when I saw that it was Bureaucrazy. And how fulfilled!

One cannot be sedately appreciative of one's own work. It was Deepak Vohra, the IFS officer turned news anchor who gave me what he called as an example of my subtle humour at its best. Chapter 9 titled "Sirrability and Seniors" in Bureaucrazy starts thus:

"*When two IAS Officers meet for the first time, there is a preliminary interval of unease while they circle around and sniff at each other's tails, trying to guess at their relative seniority.*"

"We have all felt it," Deepak said, "but the way you have put it one can only say with the poet ... what oft was felt but never so well expressed."

So when K.P.R. Nair, the dynamic owner of Konark Publishers said that there is a surprising demand for Bureaucrazy even today and something ought to be done about it, I thought of two options, one, a sequel containing all the pieces I had written about my Service in the last twenty years and second, a fatter edition of the original, with the additional material added on to it. I had to reject the first option. If a reader were to read Bureaucrazy 2, he would all the time wonder how fantastic it would be if he got hold of Bureaucrazy 1 and can hardly hide his disappointment when the bookshop told him it was out of print.

So here you are. You have *Bureaucrazy gets Crazier* which is a sequel, but not a mere sequel. You have the original too.

And rightly so. What is the use of knowing how to convoke the cretins, if you do not also master the art of sleeping without snoring? And you cannot just rely on getting an outstanding ACR. You have to win awards too.

The real masala relates to corruption. Bureaucrazy had just one chapter on Diwali shagun. From a box of sweets or a packet of Alphonso mangoes to owning a castle in Switzerland or a villa on the French Reveira is a far cry. National movements for the eradication of corruption have been started. Babas from Ramdev to Anna Hazare have jumped into the fray. So this edition has a whole section on corruption.

In all we have added 15 chapters to 31 of the first edition. So be happy.

And the book does not end in despondency and despair. In accordance with Bharat Muni's advice in the Natya Shastra, we have a sukhanta or a happy ending. As the condemned prisoner asks for a reprieve of one year in order to perfect his technique of making a horse fly, he says, "Much can happen in a year. The king may die. I may die. Or, for all you know, the horse may fly…"

Yes, dear readers, don't put on long faces. All is not lost yet. The horse may fly!!!

Praise for Bureaucrazy

"Humorous, deliciously anecdotal, incisively witty … Bureaucrazy should be mandatory reading for all aspiring and fledgling bureaucrats, for it is the quintessential guide to the Machiavellian manipulation that propel the privileged few to the dizzying heights of power, fame and lucre."

Nandhini Iyer in *The Financial Express*, 12th Dec. 1993

"Kaw has a puckish genius for seeing the lighter side of the government game. Reading his book is an unalloyed pleasure … Here we have the rare spectacle of a senior bureaucrat baring it all. The result is a rib-tickler through and through."

Ram Varma in *The Tribune*, 28th Nov. 1993

"What is harder to find is the one who would let you into the inner happenings of the bureaucratic world. For it is a charmed circle of people who call the shots while they stay behind the wings … Kaw has created a chink in that armour."

M.K. Tiku in *Hindustan Times*, 15th Nov. 1993

"He provides a hilarious and irreverent inside view of the new breed of IAS officers, Kaw's extreme felicity with language is matched only by the thoroughness with which he deals with their mis (behaviour) … The kind of book you would love to present to your friends appearing for the IAS."

Sarita Rani in *Sunday*, 12th Dec. 1993

"Kaw seems to know every trick that the babu is likely to use to cling on his seat of power … A must for all bureaucrat-bashers."

Business Today, 7th Nov. 1993

"The author holds back nothing to amuse the reader. There are numerous anecdotes which will make the book an instant seller."

D. Venkatesan in *The Hindu*, 9th May. 1995

"With a gibe here and a sally there, the author caricatures many types of people that one encounters in the corridors of power. His perspicacity is couched in words pregnant with meaning in a book that is readable from beginning to end."

Indira Luthra in *India Perspectives*, August. 1994

"One of the most readable satires recently published. The language is lucid and keeps the reader glued to the book from the first page to the last."

Gopal Misra in the *Sunday Mail*, June. 1994

"An insider's view of the goings on in the 'heaven-born' service. The book rips open the innards and exposes the malaise that afflicts the premier service … It commends itself as a Handbook for Probationers in their progress towards the pinnacle."

K. Chandramauli in *The Pioneer*, 25 Sep, 1993 and The *Economic Times*

"The book is a 'Do-it-yourself-or-someone-else-will-do-it-for-you' manual on how to get ahead of other IAS heads … The overall impact comes through as a delightful mixture of humour and insight."

P.K. Doraiswamy in *News Time*, Hyderabad, Dec. 1993

"This is the book for you: blunt and telling, irreverent, biting and sarcastic."

Omesh Saigal in *Mid-Day*, 18 Sept. 1993

"I would commend the book to all, particularly the service officers. Let them do introspection on the various aspects highlighted in a lighter vein although they are serious."

R.S. Khanna in *I.I.P.A. Journal*, Jan–Mar. 1994

"Mr. Kaw's delightful style is intelligent camouflage for the pithy nature of comment. It is the flavour that keeps the content digestible."

Captain Ali Ahmed Zaki in *USI Journal*, July–Sep. 1994

"Kaw's latest offering bares it all. It has got all they don't teach at the Lal Bahadur Shastri National Institute of Public Administration peppered with extreme felicity of language and an in depth understanding of the service in which Kaw has put in many years."

Deepika Gurdev in *Indian Book Chronicle*, Apr–May 1994

PART ONE
So The Story Goes

1

The Burra Sahib Syndrome

The ICS were the primal *burra sahibs*; that too its British members, for whom the honorific was initially coined. They were the ones who lived like lords in sprawling mansions, guzzled beer over a five-course lunch while the perspiration flowed in rivulets from rubicund face to starched collar, then lay in siesta stupor to the breeze blown by a punkah-boy, played tennis in the afternoon and bridge in the evening, and took a dusky concubine to bed.

Sovereignty vested in them, as bequeathed by the British Crown; there was no Minister, MP, MLA or *sarpanch* to share authority. Their lightest word was law, and the entire might of the state available to back up that word with lathi-blow and sword-thrust, whiplash and gunfire.

Seated on their caned thrones, they would peremptorily shout, "*Arre! Koi hai?*", for there was strewn around them a retinue of *jamadars*, *khansamas* and *chuprassies*, whose names they were too arrogant to remember. They could pretend ignorance of vernacular tongues and get by with a smattering of broken Hindustani. There was nothing incongruous in their clothiers being at Savile Row or the attempt to recreate the cliffs and downs of the emerald isle in 'little Englands' everywhere.

When Indians gained entry into the rarefied realm of the ICS, we got the brown *burra sahib*; as hermaphroditical a creature as one could conceive of. The white sahib might on occasion let his hair down and come off the pedestal, call a *khidmutgar* Raheem Bux, interject an adulatory obiter while imposing a jail-term on a half-naked fakir or learn to speak chaste Urdu. But the brown sahib, dragging his schizophrenic self, ashamed of being part of a draconian system yet proud of having penetrated into the sanctum sanctorum of the Raj, dared not make a slip. He had to speak the Queen's English, keep the stiff upper lip, display officer-like qualities, behave like a gentleman and, in general, be metamorphosed into a caricature of the real thing.

It never occurred to the brown sahib that a dark suit went off well with fair colour, for it enhanced the pale and the pink. A sable skin in a black suit just threatened to turn invisible. He could not see the incongruity of savouring civilized slivers of mango on a plate, when the fruit was meant to be held in the hand and sucked dry with ravenous lips. Or the absurdity of eating an *aalu ka paratha* and achar with fork and knife. On the contrary, he spent sleepless nights trying to master the art of munching a crisp *papad* with nary a crackle, or the greater virtuosity of breaking wind soundlessly.

Then came the great divide. Further induction into the ICS was stopped and the IAS launched as a non-colonial counter part of the erstwhile imperial service. This would have been the right time to bury the burra sahib mentality, but a great opportunity was lost. ICS officers continued to rule the roost till recent times and provided a role model for newfangled recruits to the nationalist cadre.

A few years of the pseudo-burra sahibs and the country could take it no longer. Analysis showed that the *memsahibs* of an earlier generation had spawned most of the newcomers, who tried to ape the British by watching the brown burra sahibs. Thus they were the copy of a copy, than which there can be nothing more ridiculous.

Several committees later, the Government decided on various steps to ensure induction of bright boys and girls from ordinary families, rural areas, scheduled castes and tribes, backward classes classes and so on. Getting pass marks in the interview was no longer compulsory.

It is not that it did not have impact. Quite a few children of common people came in. Had they been left alone and allowed to grow in their own natural way, these kids might have charted a new course and the country avoided the tragedy of the Burra Sahib Syndrome.

But that was not to be. Government set up the National Academy of Administration at Mussourie to instill the right values and attitudes among the probationers.

So, this Mahabir Singh from a village in Haryana was taken in hand. He ate *sarson ka saag* and *makki ki roti* and *desi ghee* using his five fingers. He drank prodigious quantities of *lassi* and *sharbat* and *kanji*. He wore a *khaddar dhoti* and *kurta*. He answered the call of nature in the wide open fields where men are men, *lota* in hand. He lived with his rustic wife Phoolan Devi and sometimes made love to her on a stack of hay or in sugarcane field.

How could this kind of man be the Collector of a District? He behaved just the way a common garden variety Indian did. Could he command respect and obedience? Why, he established in pure Haryanvi illicit relationships with people's mothers and sisters in every sentence he spoke. This would not do at all.

So Mahabir was shown the ropes, by precept, example and peer group pressure. Now he sat sedate in dinning chair, napkin in lap, elbows not resting on table, using the right fork and spoon, drinking red wine with red meat and white with white. He called for cold beer at lunch, gin and lime in the afternoon, whisky and soda in the evening. He learned to like his coffee black. He wore blue blazers, three-piece suits in brown and steel grey, cufflinks and tiepins, red silk handkerchiefs in upper left pockets. He abandoned Phoolan Devi in favour of Patricia Gomes, a dark delicate brunette from Goa. He appreciated Hari's desire to be addressed as Harry, Grover became Groovy, and Jyoti got converted into Jo Jo.

Two bright boys he begat from Patricia and they landed straight into Sanawar, where their classmates were children of business tycoons, film and sports stars, political personalities. Now their careers were assured, for they would remain on first name terms with future captains of the industry, leaders of the nation, bureaucrats and sundry bigwigs.

Mahabir lost his robust conversational style, wild, plain and turbulent; he cultivated a frigid, formal, frosty manner which did not encourage communication. Gone was his gay chatter, easy informality and natural ebullience. He became a prim, prissy, pinched-nostril kind of person, with a permanent frown on his forehead. Above all, he stopped saying "oui" if pinched; his reaction now was the more sophisticated "ouch".

Today, looking at this grey-haired, distinguished looking, potbellied, middle-aged man, one hand in trouser pocket, holding a pipe in the other, with a forbiddingly stiff exterior, it would be well nigh impossible to recognize the rustic Mahabir. He is ashamed of his family background, of the fact that his father was just an ordinary peasant and his mother an illiterate woman. He disclaims them, compels them to stay on in the village, and once when they arrived at his house while a party was on, rushed them to some inner room, hoping to hide and bury his past.

Pity this burra sahib of the 1990s. There are no khidmutgars for him to shout "koi hai" at. All power has been siphoned away from his job, but he still has the accoutrement of authority. It is he who writes the note and approves a proposal and gets the shrapnel when the file explodes. Because he is close to the political masters, he chooses to fantasize about his real importance in the decision making process.

That accounts for his nose-in-the-air attitude, his intolerable superciliousness, his taking on airs as if he hails from divine lineage while the rest are mere mortals. He deems it infra dig to socialize with the common run of humanity. It is not unusual to hear his drawing nasal query: "Which service?" at a party. If the other says, "Railway Traffic", or something to that effect, you can see his eyebrow twitch a millimeter and his eyes acquire a slightly contemptuous glaze. "Oh", he says and adds, "hmm …" and does not know what to say next and soon passes on to join a group of equals, where he might feel more at ease.

One telling indication of the image of the service in a cartoonist's evocation of a senior bureaucrat's doings in burlesque line: A comically rotund figure, overdressed in formal attire, puffing at a cigar held at arrogant angle, with smug, complacent eyes, saying no to everything, dithering, delaying, getting all entangled in ribbons of red tape, making obtuse utterances that sound sensible but are just convoluted jabber, moving in lackey-like subservience to the dhoti-clad politician, changing views with the alacrity of weather-vane, jockeying for power—that is how cartoonists see the average IAS officer.

No one can accuse them of being too far away from the truth.

PART TWO

Going Together

2

Savitri or Menaka!

The other day, I received an invitation card for a wedding. I was happy to observe that Walawalakar was getting married. After I had perused the name of the girl and drawn a blank, I naturally looked for the name of her father. Would you believe it—I just couldn't place the man. The obvious conclusion was that Walawalakar's career was finally and irrevocably ruined.

The is much too frequent an occurrence these days, and as tragic as car accidents and bride burnings. One feels so sad at brilliant and promising careers cut short prematurely, just because some chit of a girl has a shapely nose or extra large eyes. Walawalakar is in some ways a protégé and so I have done a bit of research and ferreted out the appalling truth. His intended father-in-law is a draper in Daryaganj!!!

I think the time has come to face the problem squarely and do some plain speaking. What does one expect from a wife? Is our concept so antediluvian as to dream up the scenario of a love-lorn couple holding hands on moonlit nights in scented gardens? Do we want a sari-clad Savitri or a jeans-wiggling Menaka? Should she be a good cook or a vamp with an enticing smile?

In the olden days, matters were much simpler. What one looked for was a senior man in the Service, someone around 45, with a sound heart, likely to last a decade or so and lend the helping hand so crucial in the initial years. One did not have too many to choose from, especially if one was hunting for names like Iyengar or Gangopadhyaya in the Civil List. All one had to do was to find out whether they had eligible daughters, and hey, presto! One could summon the astrologer and fix an auspicious date.

Today, the field is wider. Right at the top are money bags, who are always in power, whosoever be on the *gaddi*. With an affluent father-in-law, one may use the monthly packet for purely sundry expenses on betel-leaf and tobacco. The wife is naturally a director on several companies, and draws a not inconsiderable salary for tendering financial advice to her father or keeping his accounts. Her dowry can be conveniently coverted into investments which yield substantial dividends. The pop-in-law is apt to grant munificent gifts to his grandchildren, owing to the love and affection that he bears them. Any time one is in trouble, he gladly sorts out the matter over a glass of beer with the minister concerned or senior bureaucrat.

Next in demand are the political bigwigs. Although not so dependable, for they keep flitting in and out of power, they are much more effective as long as they last. Adept at horse-trading, they help each other's sons-in-law, lest they be accused of nepotism. It does not matter what service one belongs to. They can post a foreign service officer permanently to New Delhi, and an IAS officer to New York. An IPS officer need never hold a police job, he manages airports and tourism instead. Nor may an IAAS man be hamstrung in audit; he can be a cultural attaché in London on the specious ground that he pens passable poetry.

Trouble erupts when the politician father-in-law changes sides. If he moves over to the party now in power, there is no hassle. But if otherwise, God help the poor son-in-law. He may face a sudden suspension or at the very least a raid on his bank lockers. Someone may decide that he is holding liquor in excess of the permissible quantity, or an unlicenced weapon. If the matter is serious, opium or a stolen stone idol may be "recovered" from his house. But he can never complain of life being dull.

Among those who marry an officer's daughter, preference is invariably given to the engineer father-in-law who does not have to depend merely on salary for a livelihood. Many prefer an army officer for his ability to train the daughter in social behaviour, especially during mess dances. Very few choose the service bureaucrat. If he is a good, helpful man, he is unlikely to hold any worthwhile post; and if he wields power, it is improbable that he helps anyone save himself.

But suppose the die is cast and one has married for love, or what passes for it in the present day world. Or one has been duped into nuptial ties by one of the several headhunters who infest the environs of the National Academy. Does one say goodbye to a career?

Not necessarily. For although one has lost a lifetime chance of bagging a powerful pop-in-law, one could still count on the sharer of one's pillow.

How a charming wife is used to prop up a sagging career is best exemplified by Tukaram who was a tongue-tied thumb-twaddler and would have graced some ornamental shelf, but for his petite, garrulous wife. Depending on the type of boss he

had, she would smile demurely into his eyes, flirtatiously fill up his fourth glass of whisky or travel with him for holiday on Goan sands. Of course, he was better known as Mrs T's husband, but I never found him any the worse for this snide appellation.

Remember Sarangi, an absolute nitwit, who would have floundered on the rocks of bureaucratic politics had it not been for his better-half running the department by proxy, from his residential phone?

For his own sake, I hope Walawalakar is listening!

3
First Lady

The IAS wife is to be distinguished from the lady IAS officer, for her only claim to eminence, if eminence is the word I want, lies in the state of matrimony she has entered into. She is transmuted into a VIP just by managing to grab one of the hundred most eligible bachelors appearing in the marriage bazaar of the country each year.

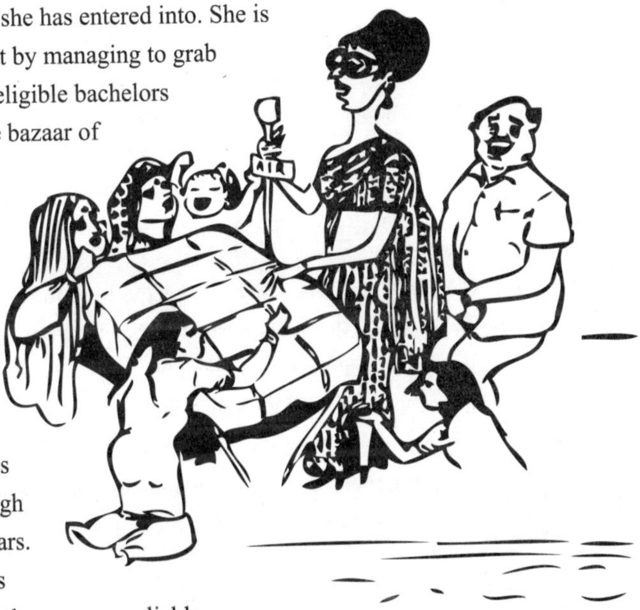

No sooner is the list of successful candidates published than a flurry of activity is witnessed on the Wedding Exchange. In our days, a dowry of seven lakhs was considered unusual enough to be talked about for years. Presently, the price tag is unmentionable. For one, there are no reliable statistics. For another, a colleague who gave out a rash figure of 50 lakhs over the TV network was ostracized by the *biradari* for days.

But in this game, money is not the only counter. Hordes of girls invade Mussourie every year in the hope that they can land an IAS bridegroom. Some camp in the little town for months on end. The boys, dressed in blue blazers with the IAS crest, are easy game. Many flirt and forget. A few philander and remember. Only a rare bird is ensnared by love, lust or blackmail.

Enough of these murky waters, The lady is wedded to the man of her choice. What ensues?

She gets her first shock when she sees the size of his pay cheque. I remember visiting Srinagar soon after selection. In those days, an IAS officer started his career with the princely sum of Rs 350 per mensem. Imagine my discomfiture when an old lady asked me what salary the Government paid me. As I hesitated, she hazarded a guess. Was it 10,000 rupees, she asked tentatively, half-fearful of hurting my feelings by quoting too low a figure. I smiled enigmatically and passed on. Any answer would have been an anticlimax.

The IAS wife wakes up from her honeymoon slumber into a ramshackle nineteenth century hovel in a rickety rural backwater, light-years away from civilization. The sole item of furniture pilfered from the office is a straight-backed cane chair, so ancient it is almost an antique. The help consists of a lugubrious lackey, stranger to any culinary skills. Vanished are her dreams of a Raj household of *jamadars*, *khansamas*, *masalchis*, *syces*, *ayahs* and *bairas*!

But there are compensations. Once she gets used to the somnolent social life, it is a treat to be so lionised. She hears hushed whispers about the SDM Saab's Memsaab and is not displeased when the granddaughter of that hoary retainer sports an inexact copy of her hair style. The BDO invites her to meetings of mahila mandals, where half-veiled village women gape at her Pochampalli saris and manicured nails, while she falters through her homily on family planning or small savings. And the way they crowd close to her for the photograph is really flattering to her ego.

A few years later, she is the Collector's wife, Chirperson of Hospital Welfare Committee, organizer of Red Cross Fair, chief guest at school annual day, beauty contest judge and presiding deity of each kitty party. There is gossip, intrigue, backbiting, fun, petty fighting, friendships and jeolousies. One or two wives invariably attach themselves to her like limpets and are referred to disparagingly as her "*chamchies*".

She lives in a huge mansion, with acres of land attached, where she grows wheat or sugarcane, banana or coconut. She has an army of servitors, attendants and hangerson. Wherever she goes, she is the First Lady, gets the best seat in the front row, is the first to be served at dinner and is the cynosure of all eyes. Though she does not know it yet, this is the high point of her life and she will always recall her district days with nostalgia.

Even at State Headquarters she is quite comfortable. A house of reasonable size, a couple of henchmen, a lawn where cane-chairs can be aired of an evening and a husband who can be depended upon to return after 7 p.m., with three boxes in tow. The phone is always ringing and she is sick of feeding lies to the public about what her husband is doing at the moment *gusal*, *pooja* or *dand-baithak*. Her children are her salvation, for they are in their difficult, adolescent phase and need her attention.

All her life she has heard of a Government of India posting and dreamt of the time her help-mate will straddle South Block and sign agreements with visiting delegations for the national news. The actual posting is a washout. For the first six months she lives off a suitcase in a single room of the local Bhavan, all her clothes dumped in the garage of an obliging friend. She moves into a two-room flat, where the drawing-room will take just one piece of a sofaset and the curtains won't fit. The bazaar is half a mile away. She sheds off the fat midriff in a trice, trudging to and fro with shopping bag, for the first time in her life actually speaking to bakers, butchers and greengrocers. The part-time help talks Tamil and the turnover is just mind-boggling.

Whenever the Department of Personnel sets up a committee to look into the reason why talented officers do not make a beeline for Delhi, they better interview the IAS wives first and listen to their interminable tales of woe.

The little woman's role in the shaping of an officer's career is really crucial. An ill-suited *begum* can cook his goose. She will accept gifts from his admirers, quite often without his knowledge, and besmirch his reputation. She may squabble with the chief's wife and create a carping critic with constant access to his ears. She may flirt with a colleague and make a scandalous scene when he is provoked into a pass. She may egg her spouse on in an unequal fight with a powerful, unscrupulous politician and lead him to disaster.

But a good wife is God's own blessing. She brings in extra bits of cash from parental coffers in times of need. Her uncle wangles a Tokyo posting for him. She makes eyes at a susceptible senior in the crucial week when his name is being considered for empanelment. She laughs at the jokes of his boss's wife and loses to her in *paploo*. She tells him with an invisible gesture when he has imbibed too much and is making an idiot of himself. She nags him in moderation so that he does not stay in the office overnight, but has no guilt feelings about an occasional evening out with the boys either. With the studied under-statement of a *shahtoosh* or a *jamawar* she conveys the subtle message to the discerning that he is the scion of a noble family. She is his sartorial adviser and is responsible for the stiff collar and the clean cuff. She keeps him sexually sated, so that he has no need to fool around and compromise himself. The list is virtually endless.

There are some officers who seek to satisfy their money-making ambitions through their better halves. Huge farms, orchards or factories are set up in the wife's name and she is projected as a successful woman entrepreneur. This is an invitation to trouble and mostly leads to a CBI raid followed by suspension.

Others persuade the Frau to seek a political career, on the premise that her clout will provide an insurance cover. IAS wives have become MLAs. MPs, even ministers, and sometimes their support has bolstered up a husband's sagging career or secured a plum posting for him. Politics is, however, a double-edged weapon and what it gives with speed it snatches away with equal swiftness, if the wind changes direction.

Even less glamorous professions create problems. A university teacher with a non-transferable job, for example, can neither give up the well-paid position nor accompany the husband in his gallivantings. The end result is prolonged periods of separation, children conceived in summer vacations and Christmas holidays, and occasional quickies stolen over weekends. Neither partner can accuse the other of cheating, for there are extenuating circumstances. Kids have perforce to be lodged in distant boarding schools and grow up as strangers to both the parents. Moneywise too, there is no advantage. Friends who have working wives have assured me in solemn tones that expenses double unproductively as income expands. And they should know.

The IAS women have a grapevine of their own. There is a strange tendency among husbands to unburden their souls of office gossip, when they take off their socks and twiddle their toes. Perhaps it is the subliminal feeling that any communication between a husband and wife is a privileged one and does not infringe the Official

Secrets Act. I have always been informed about my next posting by my wife and this is said to be the general experience.

But this is not all. Wives know what transpired behind closed doors in Cabinet meetings. They are aware of what the erstwhile Mrs *X* (since divorced) told Mr *X* in the Club Lounge. You learn that the Chief Secretary's irascibility is no reflection on your performance; he has lately had a touch of rheumatoid arthritis. The Chief Minister is unhappy with *Y* and his name had been forwarded to Delhi. And so on.

A hyperactive IAS wife sometimes tastes blood and likes it. Such a woman may start by giving the impression that she would not be averse to putting in a word with her spouse. If he is submissive, her interventions prove effective. Gradually she may decide to bypass the superfluous intermediate channel of the husband, and pass direct orders to his subordinates. Within three months, she is running the department for him, perhaps more efficiently and without any hassle. This may be good for the nation, but carping critics start talking of unconstitutional centres of power. Their peculiar thesis: Queens must be decorative pieces of furniture.

Personally, I don't agree with them. I think it would be a much better country if the wives ran it and the husbands played golf.

4

The Dharmendra Effect

Students of physics recall with fond affection how, once upon a time, a new discovery in the field of optics was christened the Raman Effect. Today, a startlingly novel finding in the ancient field of matrimony deserves a similar canonization of the filmstar Dharmendra.

Briefly stated, the Dharmendra Effect underlines the multitudinous merits of acquiring a new fashioned second wife, while the first model is still in running order.

For instance, if wife no. 1 has a long Aryan nose like the 1985 Maruti, you can go in for the 1989 model to enjoy a short snub Nepali nose. The second wife could similarly be sleeker, more accommodating, and kinder to the legs than the first.

Ever since Dharmendra took the plunge, the acquisition of a second wife has become the in thing. Matters have reached such a pass that trendy males on the fast track actually blush when introducing their dowdy ancient spouses to the trim-slim catty-chatty brand-new better halves of their competitors.

Naturally, the Dharmendra Effect has infiltrated the normally staid bureaucracy too. An instance that comes to mind is that of Chaubey, a dear friend of many years. A few years ago, while returning from Delhi, I happened to stop over at the Oasis at Karnal. Soon I found myself talking to Chaubey, but stealing a glance now and then at the female face next to him. I could not dredge out even a semblance of a memory of those features. Later, I ran across him at the local theatre, and this time I was quite sure that the lady by his side was not the Oasis girl.

Now thoroughly mystified, I placed the facts before an oracle of the service. “Hah!”, he sneered. “How typical! You don’t know? My dear Sir, Chaubey has one wife at Delhi and another at Shimla. And the one *you* talking of, she is down at the village, looking after the barley and the buffaloes.”

That bit reminded me of Sukumaran, an IPS batchmate, who nurtured his profile as assiduously as any filmstar and proclaimed himself a bachelor. Every other day, prospective fathers-in-law, daughters in tow, hunted for him and I learnt at last that he had married into a rich family. Much later, I discovered that he had discarded his rustic wife as soon as he had graduated from college teaching to the police.

Apart from keeping up with the Joneses, a second marriage has some practical advantages too. In these days of working women, it is commonplace for husbands to be transferred out, while their wives stay on at the same place. Having a second wife at the new station yields the same benefits as a sailor’s wife at every port.

I know of a person (in the private sector, of course) who has two of everything—wives, families, houses, professions. He remains with one family from Monday through Thursday and then proceeds on a business tour. The other family basks in his company for the rest of the week. They say that we of the public sector must learn the secrets of enterprise and risktaking from the *nabobs* of the private sector. This certainly is an area where we could profit by emulation.

Research has revealed that for the onset of the Dharmendra Effect the flighty forties are the most vulnerable age group. The male menopause coincides with the withering away of the mate. This is the time when the husband degenerates from the tri-weekly to the try-weekly stage, and is often put on a performance diet of roast chicken and kabuli gram. Needled beyond endurance, he is out to prove his virility.

To a man wielding power, attractive women pay court either as a price for favours that he can dole out or merely as a lark or sometimes just to test whether sex with a celebrity is any different. Such affairs are ad hoc, fleeting responses to momentary impulses and generally come to nought. Once in a while, if the woman is ambitious and the man inept, she can inveigle him into a second marriage so as to share his status or property.

Training courses are yet another hunting ground of the predator female. There is a story about a dark-eyed beauty who purveyed flirtatious glances along with the books in the library of a national training institute. And had the privilege of becoming the second wife of three senior officers for three months each in three successive courses. A hat trick indeed!

Then one cannot but recall the case of M.K. (a Hindu, who had a name somewhat like Mohan Krishen). He fell in love with a girl, but had the misfortune of marrying someone else under family pressure. Rather than act like a cad and desert the Mrs, as most of these Lotharios tend to do, he tried to persuade the competent authority to permit him the luxury of a second wedlock. When confronted with the rule book, he flashed an official looking document at the bewildered authorities. It was a nikahnama. They found to their discomfiture that the intrepid youth had gone and converted himself to Islam. Mohan Krishen was now Mohammed Karim and glibly quoted the shariat back at them.

Students of history will no doubt examine the shift in the status of the second woman, against a backdrop of the women's lib movement. There was a time when a kept woman had to rest content with the appellation of mistress, concubine, sweetheart or courtesan. This was a reflection of her economic standing, as she was dependent on the largesse of her paramour. Today, the single woman, be she unmarried, separated, deserted, widowed or divorced, with a secure job and her very own apartment, need not settle for anything less than a wifely status. Her children no longer pine for a father's name.

The Dharmendra Effect is a sign of the times, where woman is no longer a commodity. She cannot be kept. Rather, she takes her man for keeps.

5

Ladies, Gentlemen, Spinsters

That evening, there was a moment of tension when the door opened and the VIP entered. All the men got up; the ladies did not. The only lady IAS officer present vacillated for a brief second and then rose in her seat. So there we were, 20 gentlemen and one lady on our legs. It looked odd; it felt odd. Luckily, the VIP made a cool, humorous observation and the embarrassment was washed away by the laughter.

But the dilemma remains. Lady officers in the service are not always clear what the occasion is. If it is social, they are ladies and have chivalrous gallants dance attendance on them: if official, they are functionaries and kowtow to superiors.

This ambivalence is only a minor part of their problem. A major area of complications is marriage. Though we have pretensions of being modern, yet the *pratiloma* marriage where the wife is superior in status to the husband still carries an aura of transgression.

It is not uncommon to see a non-service husband attend a party, feeling like an outsider every minute of it. Condescending remarks come his way as good-natured members of the service force themselves to make conversation so as to put him at ease. Alas! Potentates of the pen have little intercourse beyond their offices and tend to talk shop. This is enough to rile any husband, however sweet he may be on his wife. Often he vows never to renew the experience.

IAS women, therefore, cling close to their consorts on convivial occasions. This provokes comment from all. The menfolk resent what they see as a chaperon-like attitude in the husband. The ladies decry the hand-holding syndrome as a display of juvenile behaviour.

There is also the tedious question of who follows whom. There are three options. They may decide to hibernate at a single station all their lives. But then they miss opportunities which could have zoomed them on to the fast track. Or they could treat the husband's activity as main and compel the little woman to follow him around. This is neither easy nor always feasible, and may instead involve protracted bouts of extraordinary leave without pay. It is unusual for the wife's job to get the primacy, especially as Indian husbands are generally practitioners of porcine chauvinism. Where wives have sought to impose their will, marriages have broken up.

The increasing awareness of such hassles makes the IAS male the ideal catch. Lynx-eyed observers have noted the different patterns of behaviour on the female of the species during the two stints of training at the National Academy. At first, they act like a lady and prefer to be chased. When they return from the district training, they can hear the clock ticking away and so take up the role of predators themselves.

Husband-hunting is a recent pastime in this country, where women have traditionally led cloistered lives and left this hazardous task to harassed parents. It involves the use of all feminine wiles which were stock-in-trade of English girls in Jane Austen's days. Coquetry, flirtation, archness of looks and silvery laughter are the evergreen techniques, as is readiness to go at least part of the way. On top of that, IAS husbands also presumably hope to hear the cry that must be cried by a pearl unthridden and a filly unridden.

With all these handicaps, it is no surprise to find lady IAS officers who have loved and lost, or never loved at all. Or perhaps they waited for the boy to make the first move, and tarried too long. As these lonely spinsters grow older, they sometimes take to religion and turn soft and mellow. But if they don't, there is a danger of their being metamorphosed into shrewish harridans. Woe betide a mere male who may have to serve under any such spitting fury!

In their official lives too, lady officers have to put up with unpalatable situations. I remember the days when a lady magistrate would make hardened police officers smirk beneath their bushy moustaches. One of them had the cheek to complain that he had felt handicapped in controlling an unruly football crowd because of his anxiety for the safety of the lady magistrate. Those days are past. With women putting on the police uniform as a routine now, one no longer hears jokes about the DM and

SP going on maternity leave just as communal tension breaks out. But there is still a mental block, a sort of unease, at banding over a district to a lady.

Probably men are not clear how to deal with a woman in an official setting. I know of *M* who got into a flap because he shouted at his Deputy Secretary while she promptly broke into tears. I remember *Z* advising me never to talk to a lady, whether a colleague or a visitor, alone. He always called his PA in to be a discreet witness. *K* got into trouble when he had long gossip sessions with a lady colleague and the whole thing culminated in a box on his nose delivered by the irate husband.

Woman are also unsure of how to behave in an official environment. Most of us bring up our daughters as soft, feminine creatures, who feel good when they are dolled up in diaphanous drapery and lots of makeup. These things go ill with high official status. So they camouflage their personality and try to look as mannish as possible. They forsake embellishment, gather the hair into a tight school-marmish bun, choose clothes of dull colours and indeterminate designs, put on oversized, horn-rimmed spectacles and paste a prim look on their face. While this does result in a forbidding personality that permits no nonsense, it robs them of femininity too.

Which is a great pity. For no one in his right mind wants women to look like men. Howsoever much we may talk of equality between sexes, we do still shout with the Frenchman: "*Vive le difference!*"

PART THREE

On The Go

6

Agenda For Ascendancy

The other day I bumped into Ramulu, the man with the eternally surprised expression on his face. He is such a sucker he lets himself be conned twice over by the same stunt.

When we exchanged notes, talking of this friend and that, suddenly the name of Mathur surfaced.

"Is it true," inquired Ramulu with his perennially inquisitive eyebrows raised even higher than usual, "that Mathur has bagged a post in the World Bank?"

I was forced to admit that it was so.

"But how?" said Ramulu with a puzzled air, "How does he manage it? How does each of his postings fall neatly into a predetermined pattern?"

Ramulu is not alone in his perplexity. The Mathurs of this world are a mystery, a miracle, even to masterminds. It is only recently that I have begun to suspect the awesome truth.

My first breakthrough came when I realized that 93 per cent of the Mathurs hailed from bureaucratic families. It was then child's play to see the secrets pass surreptitiously to the next generation, along with mother's milk. I was reminded of the historical precedent of Abhimanyu and the way he learnt the art of *chakravyuha* while still in the womb. I shall not be astonished if further research into the ante-natal behaviour of bureaucratic babies reveals that they start imbibing Machiavellian qualities at the foetal stage itself. What a head start over a non-bureaucratic baby, whose first memories may smack of academic abracadabra or satanic sports!

As the baby toddles in its nappies, it learns to use invisible techniques of making other infants bite the dust. It is nothing as brash as jiu-jitsu or taekwondo. As the tots fall again and yet again, they wonder if the floor is slippery or their shoe-soles waxed. The last person they suspect is their brother nursling smiling oh! So beatifically at them, faced aglow with kindliness and camaraderie.

And when the baby lisps its initial word, one can hear the musical cadence, so soothing to the ear, so devoid of meaning. Gradually, as it learns the numerous merits of constructive silences, one can see the emphasis change from inexact word to indefinite gesture, finally to lose itself in the arid vagueness of a shoulder shrug.

These early influences so determine the kid's personality that he is converted into a young man in horn-rimmed spectacles, outwardly naïve, quiet and softspoken, charmingly polite and well-mannered.

But this apparent Bumble has a razor-sharp mind, full of cunning and deceit, absolutely clear in his objectives, totally unscrupulous in achieving the career that he has plotted for himself.

He is educated at the "School" and at "College". All his life he will demolish upstart geniuses by a meek: "Are you from School?", as if there is no other. Or he will teach someone his place by a withering, "In College, we used to say ..."

When others are still unsure whether they would end up as airplane pilots or insurance agents, he has already taken the subject combination best guaranteed to secure a sure success in the IAS. Ostensibly a careless scholar, he mugs up his general English and general knowledge in clandestine corners. Before he has graduated he has reserved a place for himself in Rao's Study Circle—two years in advance.

The Chairman of the interview board is one of his numerous 'Uncles', who is suitably impressed with his self-effacing, suave exterior. The Director of the Mussourie Academy is another 'Uncle' who calls him home for cocktails, hoping he will marry his daughter. Keeping him on tenterhooks, he manages a high score on the Director's assessment, improving his all-India rank.

He is trained in a big district, next to a metropolitan city, so he can attend premieres of fashionable plays, film festivals, test matches. He may have a torrid affair with an air hostess or an aspiring actress, because it is the done thing, but he will commit matrimony only with the daughter of the Capulet family.

The Mathurs know how to read a Civil List, to calculate the dates of retirement of their seniors, to select the effective father-in-law and the scheming wife, and to tie the nuptial knot at the absolutely right time.

No one has to tell a Mathur which postings he should try for. He knows them by heart. In the state, he is the Director of Industries, Managing Director of the Industrial Development Corporation, Finance Secretary, Secretary to Chief Minister, Industries Secretary or Chief Secretary. At the Centre, he does not look at any ministries except those of Economic Affairs, Commerce and Industrial Development. If driven to the wall, he may consider other options but the least he wants is an "economic" ministry.

Mathur knows when to be at Delhi and when at the state capital, when to cool heels temporarily as Resident Commissioner of his state preliminary to making a triumphant entry into one of the prestigious slots at the Centre, and when to retreat sideways into a nine-month course at the Indian Institute of Public Administration.

The plotting of a career reaches its climax when he has done a year or two at the Centre. There is an economic ministership falling vacant at Paris. The India Investment Centre has an office at Tokyo. The World Bank need an Indian at headquarters. Where should he go? How should he clinch the issue? Mathur knows the answer to this ticklish conundrum.

Time passes. He has done a little over five years in a UN job, thus earning a pension. Back home, he is now senior enough to be noticed at the top. He attends the *durbar*, is seen at the right parties, calls on the centres of power of the moment with immaculate references, plays bridge with the emerging favourite in the bureaucracy and golf with friends in the business world.

His reputation at this stage is crucial, and he knows it. He has to be brilliant without treading on corns, sound yet not banal, tactful without being branded as servile and strong but not rigid.

This is also the right time to fire salvoes at aspirants to the throne. A friend in the fourth estate wonders how Atal, known to be rough and tough, can even be considered. Deep Throat has an inside tip about Jajoria being a wash-out because of his connections with you-know-who. There is a sudden spate of sensational stories about Sundaram and a sexy siren.

And so Mathur is in.

When I recount the results of my research to Vyas, a colleague who has long since degenerated into a philosopher, he sneers, "Oh, these plotters! I knew Darbari, who could recite the civil list backwards. He was aware who would retire 30 years hence and who would be around still. Poor Darbari! Where is he today?"

"Where?" I dutifully ask.

"Dead, my dear sir, what else? Was killed 20 years ago in a car crash." He pauses, letting it sink in, then resumes, "And what about Subramanyam, who always talked big and was about to be posted to the Commonwealth Secretariat or the Asian Development Bank? Where is he?"

I ask, 'Where?' knowing full well what is to come.

"Alive," Vyas says, enjoying the anti-climax, as my jaw drops, then adds, "but worse than dead. Had three of his heart valves blocked, underwent bypass surgery and is now quietly perched on the shelf. That is what comes out of plotting too much."

I want to tell him that plotting too much may, on occasion, be fatal, but not plotting at all in guaranteed to make you a non-starter. But I see that he is riding his philosophy high-horse. So I let it go.

Vyas himself has been on the shelf so long it really does not matter now.

7

The Surname Game

Those who saunter through the cocktail circuit of New Delhi are inured to the malodorous habit of name dropping that afflicts the twining climbers on the social façade. Such a one might interject, apropos of nothing, with a careless wave of his manicured fingers — "As I was telling Narasimha last evening ..." or "Manmohan mentioned at lunch today ...", leaving the deciphering of these first names to the listeners' imagination.

But a lesser noticed phenomenon is what might be referred to as the case of the Missing Surname. You are introduced to someone at a party. He looks greyly distinguished, is smartly attired and wears expensive cologne. You wait expectantly for a matching name like Kanwar Bahadur Singh Shekhawat of Shergarh or Pandit Hari Mohan Das Chaturvedi or at the very least Doctor S.N.O.B. Nanjudappaiah.

It comes as a mild shock to learn that he is a mere 'Shri K. Lal'. A veritable anti-climax. What kind of a name is that? Who is he? What is he? Where from is he?

Is he a Panjabi or a Madrasi? A Bengali or a Gujarati? You look with greater attention for those tell-tale signs. He is too fair to be a burnished specimen from south of the Vindhyas, has an aquiline nose that could never belong to the Mongoloid east, is a shade too suave to hail from the Wild Northern Climes and has a smart alecky smile tha ill goes with the staid west.

Is K the ubiquitous Krishna? And so, is he Krishna Lal Chaubey or Yadav or Sinha or Sharma or Jatav or what? If he speaks of Hindutva, what stance to adopt? If he argues about the Mandal Commission Report, should you speak for or against?

Wait! Could he be a member of the so-called Scheduled Castes, I mean Harijans? Is it that the initial K is a cowardly cover for some ghastly appellation like Khota or Kaaloo and 'Lal' added thereto as a measure of respectability?

That were madness. These days when it is proudly proclaimed that your childhood was spent mother-naked on a buffalo's back and when having attended a public school is akin to murder or some such misfeasance, no one would be ashamed of proclaiming a blue-blooded Harijan origin. One has heard upper caste boys asking with desperate urgency whether marriage with a caste or tribe would confer that coveted status on them. Or seen them spend sleepless nights mulling over sure-fire schemes of acquiring certificates of backwardness.

Some people are just plain lucky. Their parents have bequeathed them an India rubber name that is capable of being stretched in any direction. Plus they possess a remarkable penchant for making ingenious modifications to the given name, so as to suit the current circumstances.

We had an officer. God alone knows what his name was. When I met him the first time, everyone referred to him as Anang Pal Singh. I learnt later that this was because we had a Rajput Chief Minister at the time.

It was quite understandable that he called himself Pandit Anang Pal, when we got a Brahmin CM, and Chaudhry Anang Pal when we got an OBC. He got transformed to Mr Anang Paul, when we got a Christian at the top. I have often wondered what form his name would have assumed if we had a Muslim!

This is a subtler game than that. It is protective camouflage. It is an upper caste fellow trying to get rid of his surname, hoping he might be mistaken for a Harijan.

There are chaps whose father bequeathed them a fluty, tradition-rich name like Krishan Behari Lall Srivastava. But whenever they said Srivastava, Saxena or Mathur or even Trivedi or Vajpeyi, their interlocutors froze and lost their bonhomie. The accumulated awesomeness of the reputation these surnames have acquired over the past millennia was itself their undoing.

So, being worldly wise and not wanting to be dropped out in the first screening itself, they instead dropped their surnames. But even Krishan Behari Lall was a dead give-away. A devotee of the Lord Krishna in his dalliance phase could only belong to the cow belt. So they mislaid Behari on the way and shortened Krishna to a K.

And finally, they found the extra L in Lall superfluous. It was silent, yet it took space and ink and effort.

K. Lal is perfect. It is pithy. It is casteless. It is almost anonymous.

8
Godfathers Galore

The fortunate ones are born to influential fathers. A scant few choose their father-in-law wisely. For the rest of us pygmy mortals, the only course left is a godfather.

A godfather is a benevolent personage, getting on in years, who has attained a certain stature in the political, administrative, business or journalistic hierarchy, and is capable of taking young bureaucrats under his protective wing.

The godfather has to be chosen with circumspection and wooed with persistent patience. Ideally, he should be placed at an eminence with prospects of an even higher elevation, ambitious and capable of perseverance in pursuing his lofty objectives, bright but not with a luminosity that frightens away superiors, well-connected and able to encash upon relationships, rich but with no question about his integrity, jogging rapidly on the fast track yet within acceptable speed limits.

In politics, what matters is durability. In bureaucrats, one should value foresight. Among businessmen, non-partisanship. Journalists should be judged by their suppleness.

There is a recorded case of a third class graduate rising from a nondescript OSD to a high constitutional office, purely by dint of patronage extended to him by his boss over a period of 40 years. As the boss rose, so did the subordinate, placing his feet on each rung just as his godfather vacated it. This is the Staircase Effect or the classic godfather–godson relationship.

In practice, such perfection is rare to come by. What usually happens is that the elevation of the godfather and that of the favoured child are positively correlated.

It is almost as if the former pulls up the latter through the force of attraction. This connection could thus be named the Magnetic Effect.

Once chosen, the godfather has to be won over. Sometimes, he may be childless. If one can fill the filial vacuum, he will be bowled over. One evening, over a glass of whisky, in mellowed mood, he may confide his deepest desire—namely, to treat you like his own offspring. Don't shy away if he touches you. These childless fathers can be demanding in the affection that has eluded them for so long.

But if not childless, there is no reason to despair. There are other methods.

One of the most effective is to be as like him as possible. Maybe he sits late, his nerve lotuses opening towards dusk, the fragrance of his intellect spreading like *rajnigandha* in the night silence. Leaving early could then be suicidal; it would bespeak of a frivolous mind. But if you dropped by, casually and in a carelessly natural way, as if nocturnal conferences were your special cup of tea, you could score high. And then as the clock struck eleven, you might stifle an incipient yawn, speak solicitously about the lateness of the hour, draw the curtains and pack him home personally. That would be perfect.

Another method is to satisfy his desires, so that he can fulfil yours. Suppose he is a near-dipsomaniac, who starts with gin at breakfast, imbibes beer at lunch, likes his whisky before dinner and carries on with liqueurs and rum and brandy and vodka and maotai and what have you till the wee hours of the morning. What a hit you can make if you take him out on tour, with no wife to nag and no children to drag, act like a *saqi* to his Omar Khayyam and keep ladling out the stuff at no cost to him (and if you are resourceful, no cost to you either). Next time he has to recommend a name for a cushy posting or a foreign assignment, where will the choice fall? Where else!

There are a few godfathers, who seem to have no chink in their armour. They are vegetarians, non-smokers, teetotallers, impervious to the calls of the flesh and so on. But this is only a surface impression: you have to be patient in your research. Suddenly, one fine morning, you discover that he is a numismatist, a Rajneeshite, a hang-gliding bug or a Pandit Jasraj-fan. Once you know his Achilles' heel, the rest is easy.

There is a general prescription for every godfather, however impervious he might be to blandishments of other types. Good old flattery. If he has a thick black head of hair, say that he looks young and handsome, years greener than what he should be as per Who's Who. If he is grey, liken him to Rabindra Nath Tagore and say how graceful grey looks on his mature face. If he is bald, praise him for the look of distinction. If he takes after a villain, say that he would be the natural choice for a character role in a film. There is no one, just absolutely no one, in whom one cannot find something to praise, if one sets one's mind to it.

A relevant point has been raised and this is perhaps the best place to clear it up. Are two godfathers better than one? Opinion is divided on this significant issue. One school of thought holds that the best results are obtained when you stick like a leech to a single godfather. The unswerving, unflinching, non-dual loyalty that you give is repaid a hundredfold. But the post-moderns theorize that in the fluid situation of today, a more dynamic model of inter-relationships is indicated. Two godfathers are superior, if only for safety's sake. If Godfather No. 1 comes a cropper, you have Godfather No. 2 to fall back upon. The mathematical school is all for godfathers, the more the merrier, right up to 100 and beyond.

In case you decide to adopt two godfathers, it would be advisable to select them from opposite ends of the spectrum. Many states have a two-party system. At the political level, these are the CM's group and the dissident group, or the ruling party and the opposition party. Within the bureaucracy also, many states boast of a two-party system—the Chief Secretary's group and the Additional Chief Secretary's group. Having a godfather from each group has obvious merits, which need not be dilated upon.

The best bet is an interlocking chain of godfatherships, a few in politics, plenty in administration, half a dozen business tycoons and couple of journalists. Some may be formal godfathers, but quite a few could be informal ones. With some there would be family relations, that is, dinners, and children calling womenfolk of the other household Auntyji or Bhabhiji and so on. Here and there, caste system permitting marital alliances could cement the ties.Thus, over a period of time, there would be a network of relationship. And when you become successful, Ph.D. scholars would delve into these and come up with a Network Analysis.

A considerable part of the protection one enjoys as a godson stems from the mere fact of being the protégé of an influential man. Personnel Secretaries wag their forefingers at unwary Joint Secretaries who bring up audacious transfer proposals:

“Now, now, my dear. Perhaps you do not know who he is …” Ministers hesitate to administer a reproof; it might boomerang on them via his godfather, a crony of Mr X, who is close to the throne. His foreign posting comes through like a shot: “Let us do it, Sir. You know he will get it done even if we don’t agree. So why not *we* oblige him straightaway?”

A great godfather is like a ship that crosses the ocean, bearing thousands of people and tonnes of load. A politician may rise from chairman, panchayat samiti to state minister to president, youth wing to minister of state at the centre, to Chief Minister, to Union Cabinet Minister, to Vice-President and even the President of India. An entire coterie of people loyal to the man rises with him. His continuance is their vested interest. Their selfishness is his best insurance against disloyalty.

But when he falls, he strikes the ground with a thud, like an uprooted tree. And the danger is that all the little birds who have built their nests in his branches also take a tumble. When a godfather goes into oblivion, there is a sudden downpour of catastrophes on the heads of his erstwhile sons. Benumbed, they watch the calamities piling up, the commission of enquiry, the police investigation, the arrest, the suspension, the chargesheet in the court, the punitive transfer, the averted eyes of those in power and so on.

The degree of chastisement depends primarily on the degree of involvement with the godfather. As in everything else that is worth doing in life, dealing with godfathers is like walking on a razor’s edge. You have to be intimate, or else how do you become a pet. Yet you have to be aloof, for your seeming indifference will save your skin later. It is a somewhat detached involvement, in the style advocated by the Bhagwad Gita.

That Krishna should have taught the doctrine is easily understood, for he is the primeval, eternal, ideal Godfather.

9
Yea Yea, Nay Nay

They say it takes all kinds to make the world. Yes, even in as simple a matter as saying yes and no, there are six types in the Service. If not seven.

The Abominable No-man, christened long ago by palaeontologist C. Northcote Parkinson, though in a different sense, never says yes to anything, howsoever innocuous it may be. From nonagenarian precursors one has heard of this species rarer than the Yeti, but never encountered a live specimen. Perhaps, in the present ice age of unanimous acquiescence, it has become extinct.

Then we have the No-men, whom you can identify by their habit of perpetually and calmly shaking their heads from side to side, negativity writ large in small, beady eyes. They act like archaic cobras who used to guard golden chests in fairy tales. A warlike prince alone can dare do battle with these fearsome denizens of second rungs of Finance, Planning and Personnel Departments. They hiss and regret to concur. They belch forth flames and express their inability to assent.

A less dangerous breed is that of the No-but men. Like bats hiding in the dim recesses of darkness, they frighten you with sudden fluttering of wings. Shoo them away and they disappear as precipitately. They shake their heads at first, then start smiling. Good PWD, Finance and Planning Secretaries are No-but men, trained to say 'no' to their colleagues and to qualify it with a 'but' at the drop of the slightest hint from puissant politicians.

The Yes-but men are the cleverest of the lot. When a proposal is first put forward, they begin by saying 'yes'. The naive believe them and start basking in the sunshine of approbation. Then, as sudden as summer lightning, the 'but' argument strikes.

They are like scorpions who creep in unnoticed and attack when least expected. Personnel and General Administration Secretaries belong to this category.

Then we have the Yes-men proper, the most common of all. These are the yea-sayers, who nod like dolls with springs in their heads. It is a treat, in a meeting with ministers, to watch the bald and grey domes of senior civil servants bobbing up and down like "petty traffickers, that curtsy to them, do them reverence". Chief Secretaries and Home Secretaries emerge out of this mould.

Last but one, there are the Execrable Yes-men, established noddies all, who make strong, positively affirmative statements in favour of any proposition mooted by the Big Boss. These are the ones who make it a point to preface and conclude all their remarks with 'Yes, Sir!' They are the ones who stand up in their seats, even when speaking to the boss on phone. It is of such sterling stuff that Principal Secretaries to Chief Ministers and Deputy Commissioners of the CM's home districts are made.

In terms of body language, each type has its own peculiar behaviour pattern. The Abominable No-man hugs himself air-tight, arms folded dissentingly across a hairy he-man chest. The No-man does up *all* the buttons of his *bandgala* jacket and keeps his arms in the lap, right hand holding left wrist with zestful vigour, The No-but man has the top button open and his right leg rests Shirdi-like on left thigh. The Yes-but man keeps two or three buttons open, and his legs are crossed near the ankle. Some researchers are willing to categorize even a four-button open officer as a Yes-but man, but the best authorities draw the line at three. The Yes-man has all his buttons open, jacket buttons that is, and lets the knees kiss, with legs uncrossed. The execrable Yes-man can be recognized from a distance; not only are all his buttons open, and I mean *all*, but he sits with legs set wide apart, arms resting placid on top of sofa on either side.

It is strange but true that everyone has a fancy for the yes-man. There is something queerly soothing about a person who agrees with you. He rejuvenates faith in your flaccid faculties and witless perceptions. Obviously, if an objective outsider holds identical views you cannot be very much off the mark.

So you immediately recognize the exemplary virtues of the person saying yes. His heart is in the right place. His head is correctly set upon the shoulders. Every other organ is similarly situate. He has exceptional sagacity and outstanding acumen.

No-men are villains of the melodrama. Pompous asses, they rant and rave as if possessed of all the grey matter there is in the universe. In verity, they are shallow men, cocksure that right is invariably on their side. They have no depth of feeling, no breadth of vision. Inflexible to the point of being mulishly stubborn, they foolishly proclaim themselves men of principle.

Yet these may be surface impressions. There are those who hold that yes-men should be shunned, for they resemble a delicious apple looking robust red but rotten at the core. Kabir recommends that we seek out a no-man and grapple him to the soul with hoops of steel; in fact, build him a cottage in our courtyard. Many a lucky guy owes his fortune to the no-person who rests her pretty head on his pillow. The words of a no-man are likened to a medicine that tastes bitter but cures the ailment.

Perhaps, as in everything else, truth lies somewhere in the mean. The Execrable Yes-man leads a superior into the nethermost pit of hell, not daring to say 'no' even when faced with Cerberus. The Abominable No-man may draw too narrow a circle around him, warning of dangers galore the moment he steps out of line. Perhaps the Yes-but and No-but men are the most balanced. At least they possess this uncommon faculty of looking around a problem, so they can say both yea and nay.

These paragons of model conduct are not to be allowed to degenerate into the seventh category of Yes-no men, or what is almost the same, No-yes men. These are the ones who do not know what they are doing. They may say yes as easily as no. In fact, their yes is very often a no.

Take Majithia, for instance. When anyone approaches him for a favour, he says: "Yes, of course, of course ..." and forthwith rings up the person concerned. The moment the fellow leaves, he makes a second call cancelling what he had said before "Oh well! the chap was sitting with me. Had to phone, you know ..."

Sometimes, he tells the caller effusively that he (the caller) can go and meet so-and-so, as he (the officer) would have spoken to him (the So-and-so). But he never does. If the caller returns to enquire, he greets him with "Oh! Didn't he tell you I had spoken to him? Well, well, well ..." and his voice trails off into silence while his face retains its careful mask of candour and consideration, and rolling eyes insinuate meanings that are beyond comprehension.

10

Sirrability and Seniors

When two IAS officers meet for the first time, there is a preliminary interval of unease while they circle around and sniff at each other's tails, trying to guess at their relative seniority. Mere age is no guide, for a promotee is older but not so senior. Hair does not help either in these days of premature greyness and chemical dyes.

The dilemma is whether you are to sir or be sirred, to patronize or be patronized.

There was one Sinha in our batch who, so an apocryphal account goes, went around the clubs holding out his hand, "I am Sinha, IAS 1964. How about you?"

Not everyone can afford to be that blatant. People of refinement try the time-tested technique of gently dropping the name of a batch-mate in the other's cadre and letting him catch on. But persons with short memories or large cadres may not even recognize cadre-mates. With such absent-minded dopes desperately dying to place themselves, it is but humane to express the unutterable.

Seniors often ride high horses, talking down their supercilious noses to junior colleagues and mouthing stupidities with an air of rare wisdom. They autocratically assume the reins of conversation and deliver sonorous monologues to respectful audiences. The others are supposed to laugh at butchered jokes, commiserate with their corns and nod sagely at each wisdom-pearl.

Brain storming sessions frequently degenerate into long hours of lectures and reminiscences on the part of seniors. The juniors boil and seethe inside while maintaining a calm exterior. Like the blondes of whodunits they have to act dumb.

A senior is always supposed to know better. This superiority has nothing to do with his IQ which might be subnormal, or his experience which might be lopsided. He is senior: ergo, he is a know-it-all.

It follows that one never contradicts one's seniors. This results in ludicrous situations. A, the juniormost, makes a proposition. B, senior to A, proceeds to tear it to bits with all the sarcasm and wit of which he is master. Suddenly C, senior to B, intervenes and supports A's point of view. B stops in mid-stream and starts wagging his tail. The volte-face is immediate and unblushing. No one smiles. Only A, if he is very green, may permit himself a smirk on the invisible side of his face.

A favourite game which seniors play is: In-our-days-it-was-never-like-this. Their days are alluded to in hushed tones, much as one would refer to the Satya Yuga in scriptural texts. The impression conveyed is of a hoary past, hazy in the mist of myth and legend, which probably never was. In those days, civil servants were listened to with veneration, the political masters did not dare overrule them and right overcame might. Those were the days of giants, political and bureaucratic, or so we are persuaded to believe.

The senior loses no opportunity of driving home a moral. His own conduct has at all times been beyond reproach. He never refused a difficult posting; on the contrary, he would volunteer for desolate deserts and sequestered solitudes. At no stage did he suggest a trip abroad. He was allergic to five-star hotels. In short, he was a good boy.

This professed idealism slips off the oily outer skins of cynical juniors. They launch private investigations and dredge up interesting relics from his past. How phone calls from Delhi determined the pattern of his postings; how no one would accept him in a district till he soft-soaped five MLAs into taking a deputation to the Chief Minister; how rules were bent to curtail his cooling off period; how he wrangled a stint with an international organization when his brother-in-law was Cabinet Secretary and so on.

The greatest weapon the seniors wield is the annual confidential report. It is a loose sally of the imagination on the general qualities of subordinates. No allegation can either be proved or disproved. It thus tends to be a whimsical resume of sub-conscious responses.

The rating does not depend entirely, or even primarily, on first-hand experience. There is a grapevine which builds reputations or wrecks them. As two seniors munch their daily bread, one remarks, "Khobragade seems to be intelligent", and looks tentatively across the spinach. The other says, "Yes, but not very diligent." And with this curt disposal of Khobragade they pass on to international affairs and the latest nostrum for baldness.

About the sirrability of seniors, there are two schools of thought. In our days (if I may say so), we did not sir a colleague unless he was at least six years senior. Of course, this non-sirring was resorted to with great trepidation. I remember having a furious discussion in the juniors' lunch room that we should call Vaishnav, four years our senior, by his first name. There were bets that I dare not do it. We entered his room just as he lighted his post-prandial cigarette. And then, not to make a mystery of it any longer, I did utter his first name, though with a thudding heart.

Today, I find that sirring has become cheap. Juniors do not take chances. They sir persons even one year ahead, just in case. Sometimes, they sir even their juniors. My silver hair has often made me an unwitting recipient of such unmerited deference. I cannot say I blame them. With the pattern-less postings of today, one is never sure who would be the boss. There is really no point in taking uncalled for risks.

With tense senior–junior relationships, it is important to have release mechanisms. One outlet is the juniors' lunch-room where curses and swear-words make the fur fly. Another is the annual service week, during which juniors usually present a skit seeking to lampoon the seniors. The sarcasm is mild and ineffectual, but the public reversal of roles does provide a catharsis. Amidst the forced guffaws the seniors look at their own faces as in a concave mirror.

But the all-pervasive nature of seniority stands revealed when, immediately after the skit, officers line up outside the toilet in the strict order of their seniority.

11

Hearty and Loud and Thunderous

Not long ago, I met this youthful officer Das at a club. He was trying ineffectually to submerge his grief in a bottle of rum. A little sympathy brought forth the confession that his boss had awarded him an adverse entry in the annual confidential report.

The fellow was mystified. He had slogged, slaved, literally sweated on the job. Nor had he ignored the deeper, more profound aspects of official life. He had dangled the boss' infant grandson on the knee, and paid tributes to his daughter's perspicacity. He had played *paploo* and babbled *bhajans* with him. But obviously there was something he did not know, something he had not done. What could it possibly be, he fretted, clutching a fifth large in feverish grip.

I saw at once that Das was a man of the finest breeding, had received the most admirable training and had imbibed excellent work-attitudes. It was equally clear that he had mucked up something momentous. A Sherlock Holmes might have been stymied by this impenetrable mystery. I was baffled for just a few seconds.

I asked his boss's name. I looked at the young man's thin, pinched, serious lips. Suddenly I knew what the score was. What was wrong with thc whole scenario.

There are a number of bimbos in the Sevice who imagine themselves to be anointed avatars of Bernard Shaw and Oscar Wilde. Witticisms, epigrams, jokes rise unbidden to their lips and they love to see men chortle till they turn purple.

Now if such a one, deep in drollery, is the boss and he drops the manna of his wit in the arid sands of dry, dense humourlessness of such a one as my young friend, the result can be disastrous. There would be a pregnant silence while the boss waits for the guffaw, and the youth tries to make sense out of what appears to be meaningless chatter.

Very early in life, one has to learn how to laugh. It will not do to simper, weakly snigger or put on an impotent smirk. It has to be a belly laugh, a horse laugh, something hearty and loud and thunderous.

There used to be a Chief Secretary who had just one amusing story in his repertoire of reminiscences. It was long and he made it seem longer, with numerous halts and stops, going back and catching a thread and then hurtling jerkily forward, in a clutter of confusion. He must have narrated it a hundred times in my hearing. I do not recall how I responded to the second edition or for that matter the forty-fifth. In those days, I could not even conceive that one's reaction to a joke was of such serious consequence as to be no laughing matter.

But I do remember a colleague who was the old man's favourite, and the way he listened to the oft-told tale. At the launching pad itself, he would freeze into immobile attention, mouth slightly agape with anticipation, eyes alight with interest, body bent forward in avid anxiety to gulp down each tiny detail. Not by a gesture or movement did he betray that he had heard it before. He looked at the CS, virginal innocence writ large on his face, as if it was the first time.

And when at long last, with lot of puffing and wheezing, the ancient steam engine reached the punchline, what a response! As if the blue Himalayan sky had been suddenly overpowered by thick, rumbling clouds. That young man went into peals of lively laughter, with a high, reverberating sound, till tears came to his eyes. It was as if he had never heard anything so ludicrous before.

He had powerful lungs which took in a bellyful of air. So his laughter was lusty and loud. After everyone else had subsided into silence, he would continue to guffaw and giggle, stop for a second and then start chuckling all over again, as if the very memory of the narrative tickled him afresh. He would ostentatiously pull out a large handkerchief from his pocket, wipe his eyes and clear his nose. And then go into a renewed bout of jocund jubilance.

It was but natural that the Chief Sec loved him and showered choice postings on him. I can now see it from his point of view. Many of us must have worn martyrlike expressions on our fatuous faces during the tedious narrations and heaved ill-concealed sighs of relief at the bitter end. Against that dark background of somnolent sufferers, this bright-eyed boy must have shone with an angelic light. He understood, he appreciated, he applauded. Therefore, he had to be a genius.

To come back to Das. Having diagnosed the malady, it took me five seconds flat to prescribe the remedy. Laughter, I said with all the aplomb of a budding consultant who has just stumbled on a panacea, was the best medicine. I believe this to be a most original statement and plan to have it registered against the inroads of copycats and plagiarists.

12
Of Brinjals and Birbals

Shakespeare said the last word on flattery when he made Decius say about Julius. Caesar:

But when I tell him he hates flatterers

He says he does, being then most flattered.

This is the *maha-mantra* of sycophancy. The veteran toady starts his *aalaap* of adulation with this prefatory remark. He is a blunt, forthright person, notorious for an acerbic tongue. He detests obsequiousness. And he also knows the other's character—his austere, stem personality that abhors anything even remotely smacking of soft soap. But he is helpless. He can no longer remain silent. He has to speak out.

Everyone likes to be eulogized. Even a scarecrow of a hag, with pockmarks on her face, wants to be considered winsome. As officers, we may be extraordinarily outstanding in our own estimation, but another person's affirmation of these virtues is something else altogether.

There are some who counsel caution. They fear the harridan will see through the game and may even construe it as deliberate affront. Or, that an officer whose merit you extol will catch you by the collar and wag a finger at you, saying, "Now, now, now ..." in gentle reproof.

All this is the play of an over-wrought imagination. People with decades of experience will share with you their pragmatic insight. No one will stop, no one upbraid you. Nor will anyone slap your face or clamp the mouth shut. As you warm up to your theme you will see the other relaxing, becoming expansive, looking at you with rapt attention, wondering where you have been all these years. You will witness a sudden change in his demeanour, as if he has rediscovered you, unearthing depths of intelligence which he had never suspected.

So, flattery is a medicine with no negative side effects.

Some tyros pose a puerile question about the quantum of buttering up that is safe. In short, whether to lay it on thick or keep it thin. This is the kind of drivel one asks before starting anything new, be it jiu jitsu or Chinese checkers. Most of us are too shy even to get going. We are so self-conscious about the whole thing that our eyes pop out and the ears go red, and so we give away the game. The secret is to keep a straight face and lay it on as thick as you can make it, the thicker the better. After all, if too much causes indigestion, you cannot be the victim.

Persons who inquire what the subject of flattery should be need not make the effort. Is there anyone at all in the whole world in whom one cannot see something to acclaim? It could be a head of falsely black hair, a nose he thinks looks Greek, or putting dexterity demonstrated on the drawing room carpet. Artistic potential as revealed by avant-garde doodling on slipbooks, bathroom crooning or air-castle building could invite unstinted applause. One might admire stolen witticisms, original thoughts bordering on pottiness and reminiscences of events that never occurred. A double-faced villain could be complimented on his ability to look at both sides of a coin.

In India, women are never to be praised for their beauty. If unmarried, there is the danger they might misconstrue an innocuous remark as a proposal for marriage. If married, the jealous husband might pull out a revolver and challenge you to a duel. Only very old spinsters well past the age of matrimony may be safely commended for their elegant charm.

Nubile virgins can be told they are looking “smart”. This word is so vague as to encompass several meanings. It could refer to their comeliness, dress, deportment, intelligence, worldly wisdom, anything!

Children should be lauded for their scholastic ability. Every father, and especially every mother, feels highly elated if any approbatory remark is directed at the offspring. Resourceful officers, therefore, always speak of genetic factors playing a crucial role and how the children of two geniuses are bound to be prodigies.

In this process, pets are not to be ignored. As one is escorted to the living room, the first encounter is with a fluffy spaniel. Is one sure of its sex, lineage and favourite foods? Does one greet it by its first name, tickle it under the chin and offer it a choice tidbit? Does one remember to call the cat 'a cute little thing' and wonder where it got that peculiar shade of green in its eyes? Or if it is a parrot, does one pay it a formal visit, gravely offer it a green chilly and cry "Mithhooo …" in a shrill screech? If not, one has missed out on a master technique for winning over the esteem of one's superior.

In the office, flattery assumes a million hues. A boss who has acquired notoriety for the empty froth of his chatter can be called "a gifted speaker". A desk-bound dictator of dozen-paged notes could well earn the sobriquet of "draftsman extraordinaire". One could refer to a gallivanting, inveterate tourist as "an officer in intimate touch with ground realities".

A simple method for worming your way into someone's favour is to decry his predecessor. The conversational gambit starts with: "Ever since you have taken over this department, Sir …" and goes on to narrate the French Revolution that has overtaken this sleeping bastille since. "There is no comparison, Sir," you insist, proud to display your knowledge of English, "it is a total contrast." This demonstration of loyalty becomes all the more impressive in the presence of a third party. You pretend you are are talking separately to him, as if the boss is not present. "Since the day Sir has come, our working has been totally transformed," you say in hushed whisper, as if revealing a state secret.

Never miss an opportunity for fulsome narration of his virtues in a public forum. "If we as humble employees of this Ministry have achieved anything at all, the credit does not go to us," you pontificate in sonorous tones and pause for the dramatic effect. "Then to whom?", the audience seems to ask. You point with outstretched finger at your boss sitting with a smug smile on his fat face and declaim, "It is only because of *his* dynamic leadership and systematic guidance that we have arrived here. If it were not for him …" and much more in the same vein.

It was in some such setting that I once heard a colleague Sheriff holding forth on the laudable virtues of his superior Jha. When the latter's turn came, he made the usual self-deprecatory noises: "I am afraid I do not deserve all the kind words that have been spoken about me," etc, etc. And then Sheriff made a remarkable comeback that I will never forget. In his vote of thanks, he said, "Just now Mr. Jha wanted to know what he has *done* for us. Sir, I want to tell every one here. Just think. What does the sun do in the morning? What does it *do*? Apparently, it *does* nothing. But when it rises, the world wakes up, plants come to life, people start moving." He turned towards Jha and bowed, "Sir, you are like the resplendent Sun."

Wise people know that a boss, like the proverbial customer, can never be wrong. If he is of the chicken-munching-beer-guzzling variety, they sing the virtues of the good life. If he plays golf, they discover the rare subtlety of this noble pastime. And if he sings devotional songs at the sacred feet of a hypocrite holy-man, they join him in the pursuit of the life divine.

Akbar once said he hated brinjals and asked Birbal about his views on this momentous issue. Birbal said he abhorred the abominable things. Next day, Akbar announced that he loved brinjals. Birbal said he adored them. Akbar accused him of double talk. Not at all abashed, Birbal clarified that he was the servant of the Emperor and not of the lowly vegetable.

That is the kind of mental stance you should cultivate if you wish to be an Emperor's pet.

13

The Tactful Half-Smile

I do not know why they decided to field me, for I have never been particularly renowned for artfulness. This powerful opposition MP had occupied the best room in the Circuit House and he had to be shifted to accommodate a VIP. He could chew off a head just for salad, and I was warned to be diplomatic.

"You mean you want me to get out", thundered the MP "Sir, no, sir", I bleated with what I hoped was a winning smile, "we entreat you to shift to equally good accommodation". I thought the "equally good" bit was a gem.

"Really?" he sneered, "then let your blooming VIP stay there." With that he shut the door in my face with a bang of finality and I retreated, tactfully.

Gogoi tells me of the time he was Deputy Commissioner of a district and the Chief Minister came on a visit. A stranger to his fancies, he gave the posh suite to the CM and arranged the others in the pecking order. The lady doctor in the entourage got assigned a room near the kitchen.

The moment the CM arrived, he took Gogoi aside. "And where have you placed this young lady?", he queried, patting the nearer shoulder of the medico with avuncular affection.

When Gogoi disclosed the unsavoury truth, the CM. walked away in a huff. One of his PAs managed to blurt out in a whisper, "Sir, her room is always next to the CM's". Only then did Gogoi realize the amplitude of his gaucherie.

Tact is of two kinds—verbal and situational. Verbal tact consists of saying something unpleasant with an engaging smile on one's face. Situational tact could be described as retreating gracefully from a disgraceful situation.

The most hurtful word in the dictionary is the two-letter word "No". So people devise different ways of declination.

The most tactful are those who have taken a solemn oath never to say "no". Not that they do what they say. They just string people along.

Then we have those who seem to be saying yes, while actually saying no. "I want to do this and I probably will. Please be assured that I shall study the case most carefully. If I can do it, I will do it."

There are also the apologetic ones. "*You* have asked me to do this. Can I *ever* refuse you anything? It is just that in *this* particular case, I am helpless."

Others give full-blooded explanations. "You see the first proviso to sub-section 2 of section 13 does permit the grant of licence. But that proviso applies only to rural areas. In the present instance we have to be guided by the second proviso … ."

There is no dearth of friendly advice too. "We can do this, but it will be an exception to the general rule. That means a Cabinet decision. I know how close you are to the boss. You may not like to embarrass him for this trivial matter."

Some postpone the event, in the hope they would be gone by the time it comes up again. "This is an excellent idea; but perhaps the timing is not right. Now if we could defer this by a year, it might make all the difference … ."

A very adroit way of avoiding an unpleasant situation is to pretend you are dense. "Really? How interesting! Well, you see, perhaps you could leave these papers with me. I will try to wade through them once again. Maybe, the second time … ."

I am told in olden days there used to be chaps who entered what Bertie Wooster would have called the *nolle prosequi* without batting an eyelid: "Sorry, old man! I don't think this can be done." Such brash staters of the bald, inexpressible truth would nowadays be eliminated during the period of probation, if any specimen managed to smuggle himself past the eagle-eyed Interview Board.

As for situational tact, I am reminded of Kulkarni, a wizened stalwart who had risen from the ranks. When I had just joined service, I was given the onerous task of demolishing a three-storey building in a metropolitan city. Entering the narrow, devious lane my small posse found itself threatened by a thousand-strong mob brandishing guns, spears and lathis. Rushing to a nearby phone I rang up Kulkarni, my immediate superior. He promised to send reinforcements, report to the L.G., visit the spot and so on. Six sweaty hours later, no additional force had arrived. Then he rang up. "Where are you, Sir? When are you coming?" I whined. "Don't worry, my boy," he said, "I am watching the situation … from the police station."

I also remember Trivedi, a famed bureaucrat, start moving towards the exit when a law and order situation was just about to erupt into a bloody riot. "Sir, sir," I shouted with the new-found enthusiasm of a novitiate, "Where are you going? What are the orders?" He looked through me as if I wasn't there and told his driver to rush. Later, he claimed he had not foreseen the rumpus would take place so soon and had hurried to fetch the soldiery.

Such episodes lead the wag to counsel presence of mind and absence of body.

But suppose one is caught in the midst of a situation and the exit route is blocked. How to deal with it tactfully?

The safest course is to yield and win them over. The Government will yield in any case, so why should the credit not go to you?

If tact is that simple, why is it so rare? The reason is that mere yielding is not enough. It should not look like a rout.

One could say, "Look, I promise that all your demands will be conceded. You will not work more than five hours a week. Your salaries will be doubled. We will give you bonus for the period you have been on strike. We will chargesheet the chaps who remained loyal. But, for God's sake give us a face-saving formula. Withdraw the strike unilaterally today, and I shall announce all these concessions tomorrow."

Retreating gracefully also implies retracing one step at a time. "Okay, we will order an enquiry. It will be a departmental enquiry, of course. We won't shift any officer … ." Half an hour later: "Oh, all right. It will be a magisterial enquiry. We will transfer the S.P. to Armed Police." After a decent interval, the tune may be altered to: "A judicial enquiry? Right, we shall order one. You want the S.P. to be placed under suspension? Okay, we will suspend him." But then you should insist: "Now, look here. As you go out, you must shout slogans of CM. Sa'ab Zindabad."

Tact is contagious. I remember the early days when one met candid officers now and then. One of them would say in a meeting. "But, Sir, please consider the long-term effects of what you are suggesting." Today, a remark like that would at best merit a withering, "My dear boy, remember what Keynes said. In the long run, we are all dead."

These days, we have all grown tactful. The Home Secretary's car is stopped by rioters. The cops look at the scene with unruffled calm. The tyres are deflated. The Home Secretary is forced out of the car. His face is blackened with tar. He is seated on a donkey. The rioters dance a ritual dance around him, mouthing obscenities.

There is a tactful smile on the Home Secretary's face. And responding to it are the tactful half-smiles on the face of the force.

14

Braggadocio In I Major

A lesson many people learn too late can be summarized in a one-line aphorism: 'If you don't blow your own trumpet, no one else will'.

How can other people learn what you are doing? Some visionaries think that the reputation of silent hard work is like the slow fragrance of a rose which does not need the beat of a drum.

Nothing is more untrue. The dusty, musty chores of officialdom block the olfactory nerve so effectively as to let tender scents waft away unsmelt, unnoticed. None of your superiors has the time to halt in the midst of a hectic afternoon and mull calmly over the merits of his subordinates. To him, each minion is a half-visible blur, a whirling cog. Thus the need to blow one's trumpet.

The basic prerequisite is a gift of the gab. The tongue-tied moron who finds it troublesome to open his mouth and let a trillion words tumble out like a frothful cascade can write himself off. He will never be a celebrity. Most people do possess some native skills at manipulating sound, but these have to be honed to a fine sharpness through constant practice.

Thus one could, Demosthenes-like, go to a seashore, if one were handy, and out-shout the garrulous waves. Even a forest or a desert would do, the main purpose being to try mouthing nonsense at a non-audience. If the vast deeps take it, one might essay small driblets at unimportant assemblages of the *hoi polloi*, who half-hear everything in any case. And so on, by stages, to persons of increasing importance, and finally the boss.

A quality one should not have in excessive measure is modesty. Your egoless, humble acolyte of self-effacement is never conscious of doing anything great. His deprecating shrug demolishes even a fantastic first with "Oh, it was nothing … ."

The best way to blow one's trumpet is to denigrate the fellow who had the misfortune to be one's predecessor. Oh, what a mess he had created! There was no method in his madness. For full five years, he had fattened his arse, sitting on issues. He was a petty, puerile procrastinator. He never came to office on time. Nor did anyone else. How much effort you had to make merely to reestablish norms. The accounts were in arrears. Decisions were verbal. Advances were unadjusted. Policies were unenunciated. The staff had become unruly. Why, a thousand files had been found in his room alone, the oldest of them lying there for a full 31 months. And his escapades! There was so much talk about him and Miss So-and-so. Of course, one never allowed anyone to gossip. But there it was … .

And so on. The snag with such narratives is their unmitigated negativity. A listener is apt to be bored with the leitmotif of unadulterated pessimism. The skilful trumpet-blower changes the theme ever so often, interweaving the gloom with tuneful patches of what he has done since. The face-lift to the office, the removal of almirahs from the corridors, the placing of flowerpots and paintings in strategic corners, the destruction of old, unwanted papers, the surprise checks, the quick disposal, the finalization of accounts in record time, the bringing out of a policy frame and a perspective plan, the management information system, the office automation, the computerization programme, the way profits have zoomed since he took over, and much more in the same vein.

Experienced glib-talk specialists impart variety to the trumpet-blowing scenario by organizing visual demonstrations of their performance. Every little thing is inaugurated, be it a building, a facility, a cell, a book or a campaign. A VIP is summoned for the function. Naturally, he wants and gets press, radio, TV coverage. He is happy and so is the man who invited him. At the end of the visit, an album is presented to the VIP, showing his benign hands cutting the tape, his benign face beaming at the camera, interspersed with photographs of the department's excellent performance. The subliminal impact of such visual juxtaposition has been experimentally gauged as "alpha plus".

Another useful tool is the presentation, where the achievements are highlighted before a select audience. In the olden days, this was done through a lecture. Then came the charts. Later it was the slide projector. Today, it is a video film. Professional firms do it for a neat packet, but the results are astonishing. The chief merit is that someone else is blowing your trumpet, in a sombre, clipped tone which lends an air of objectivity to the appraisal.

But when the chips are down, there is no substitute to blowing one's own trumpet. Entering the room of the superior like a blizzard, one talks nineteen to the dozen and leaves like a tornado. The impression sought to be conveyed is that of a person in a hurry, eager to get things done, with too many things on his mind and breaking the speed limits with impunity. The semblance of being fast puts one on to the fast track.

One talks of obstacles and how these were successfully surmounted, of objections and how these were got overruled, of a slowmoving file and how it was transported personally from desk to desk in order to meet a deadline. Facts, figures, statistics, percentage growth rates spout forth from fluttering lips with incredible swiftness. One shows extracts from articles in newspapers and magazines, extolling the results. There are quotes from people who matter. And before the boss has time to react or ask questions, one has left.

Leaving behind a blindingly bright portrait of a young man (or woman) on the way up.

15
Inkblots On The Nose

There was this bloke who impressed everyone as a keen, indefatigable worker. He had never been with me, but somehow I had the liveliest vision of the back-breaking toil he undertook. One day, I happened to compare notes with his immediate boss and was horrified to learn that he was a malingerer.

This set off a turmoil in my mind. How had I misjudged him so completely? Next time around I refused to be overawed by the total impact of his personality and analyzed each little detail that stood out.

He wore a marked stoop, as if weighed down by the care of office. There were deep scowl-scars on his forehead and crows' feet under the studious eyes. He carried a thousand-page file. There was an open pen in his hand and inkblots on his nose. No wonder he had me fooled!

I also recall Takkar, who had the image of being a tough guy. We were so scared of him that I know youngsters literally pissed in their pants at the mere mention of his name.

Today, I can see that he had built up the myth with studied design. He remained aloof and inaccessible. You dared not step straight into his room. He had an officious Head Clerk (Personal) who claimed Takkar did not have a moment to spare in the next seventy two hours. If we proclaimed an emergency, the appoint-ment was fixed at 2130 hours. In meetings, he was rough and abrasive. He could raise blisters on the heart with a slight swerve of his tongue. A favourite ploy of his was to send memoranda conveying displeasure, through a liveried minion who drove you out of bed at 3 a.m. and made you sign a groggy receipt. He never sanctioned casual leave without forcing you to grovel on bended knees.

When I met this hard nut a few years later, I was flabbergasted to find him a shy old fuddy-duddy with a heart that could melt like butter on a frying pan.

Talking of images reminds me of Neelam, a girl whom everyone regards as a dynamic go-getter. I too thought so till I came across this book on myth-building, which taught me to rethink first impressions.

When I started analyzing the overall effect of breathless speed that I associated with Neelam, I realized with a shock that this was due to the sheer physical impact of her jet swiftness and glib chatter. She entered a room as if a tornado had swept in. When she left, one felt a typhoon pass out. She talked nineteen to the dozen, without pausing to take breath. Above all, she spoke with unblushing immodesty of what *she* had done and what *she* planned to do. She talked with conceit of her achievements which she thought were unprecedented and unrepeatable.

Then we have the classic case of Mittal, whom I always regarded as the most resourceful chap I ever met. You buzzed Mittal at midnight for a seemingly impossible task, and lo and behold! it was done. He never said no. He did not point out the difficulties of an assignment. He said quietly that it would be done, and unobtrusively and promptly did it.

Imagine my surprise, therefore, when I met a poor relation of mine and he launched into a veritable tirade against Mittal. Of how he had called on him a hundred times for a piffling matter, but to no effect. I could not believe my ears. I rang Mittal up, and next day the work was done.

This aroused my curiosity. Just a wee bit of research revealed that Mittal's reputation rested on the principle of selectivity. He had a short list of politicians and officers who mattered. Anything they said was top priority and attended to with lightning speed. (It just so happened that I was Principal Secretary to the Chief Minister those days.) As far as the general public was concerned, it could as well go to hell.

Then there was Subramanian, who impressed us all with his phenomenal knowledge of events, national and international. In meetings he would reveal, in incredibly offhand manner, how petro-dollars were affecting the economy of Saudi Arabia, or what the last CIA Director had confessed in his autobiography. I am talking of the days when the glossy magazines had not yet made their appearance in India. Gifted with a prodigious memory, he would reel off statistics of gem and jewellery exports, suicide trends or divorce rates. The passages of power resounded with tales of his superabundant perspicacity and superhuman omniscience.

Only later, when I came close enough to look over his shoulder, did I realize that his fabulous image emanated entirely from a private subscription to *Time* Magazine and the *Economic and Political Weekly*.

Khan is another outstanding example of how appearances are stage-managed. As chairman of a public sector undertaking, he had the awesome reputation of never having been criticized. No newspaper headline besmirched his name. No legislator spoke of him except in glowing terms.

This made me curious. I found Khan singularly ingenious in his methods. Show him the man and he could tell you how he might be pleased. One was made happy by offering employment to his brother-in-law. Another just wanted a dozen transfers to be made at his behest. A third needed nothing more than a bottle of whisky every month. Yet another was content if advertisements were issued to newspapers through his wife. The fifth asked for a benami contract that yielded a steady income. One fellow did not require anything except an expensive suit-length at Diwali. Then there were chaps who liked to be invited to parties, guys satisfied with a leather purse with their initials monogrammed on it, and persons lugging giant-size egos and mollified just by the word 'Sir'.

I would like to conclude this catalogue with Bhattacharjee, generally regarded as indispensable wherever he served. When I made a surreptitious study of his modus operandi I found it to be astonishingly simple.

All he did was to filch away the vital files and lock these away in his personal almirah. Access to this was restricted only to him and a hand-picked PA. Every time there was a crisis, it was he who was summoned, for he held the key to indispensable information. If he ever felt that his importance had gone unrecognized, he proceeded on leave on the eve of a significant event, pretending to fall suddenly ill. The resultant near-fiasco at once established his cardinal criticality to the organization.

16
The Grapevine

The other day, I called on Shantaram, a colleague posted in a Ministry across the Vijay Chowk. I found him distraught, with dark rings under the eyes. A solicitous inquiry revealed that he was under terrible pressure from his boss. A few more months and he would break down.

"But your boss is going," I said.

"What?" he cried, astonishment writ large on his gaping, dropped-jaw face. "Where? How do you know?"

"Well," I replied, with pardonable smugness, "A little bird told me. It is supposed to be hush-hush. The PM signed the file only 'ten minutes ago. He is going to Asian Development Bank."

"Hurrah !" he said and pumped my hand up and down, "let us go out and celebrate."

The point I am making is the simple one that in bureaucracy you cannot survive if you do not have an ear to the ground. For, strange as it may seem, the grapevine sprouts and spreads in subterranean channels.

Lest we commit a basic blunder, it is good to remember that there are only five grapevines out of the infinite ones existing in the universe which are of immediate interest to us. These were the officers' wives', personal staff's, journalists' and the bazaar varieties.

The officers' grapevine subsists on loose-tongued gossip-loving durbari kind of bureaucrats, who revel in listening to tittle-tattle and in retailing half-baked rumours.

They breeze into the office around half past ten, sign away the few files that have strayed on to their table, ring up half a dozen friends for the latest, stroll out to a few key Ministries for personal contact, have lunch with an industrialist with connections in high places, and reappear in their place of work around four for a signing spree and a dozen phone calls. Even their private life is devoted to the assimilation of gossip. They start early at the golf course and continue in the evening at the cocktail party, wedding reception, bridge foursome, quiet drink, social call and what have you.

The wives have to depend entirely on their husbands for the lowdown. Some husbands talk in their sleep, others on the pillow, still others after a bout of sex. Quite a few have no other topic and are compulsive talkers. Intelligent women can draw out the taciturn by clever questioning. But as soon as a wife gets to know anything juicy, she cannot keep it to herself. The moment her husband's back is turned she rushes to the phone to tell her ten best friends. Wives meet in the kitty, coffee, mango, *dahi-bhalla*, *aalu-chaat*, birthday and other kinds of parties, and constantly exchange inside stories. They are incapable of straight narration and garnish the tales with lot of *masala* and histrionics.

Returning from their jaunts, they swoop upon their unsuspecting spouses and inundate them with every scandal, tit-bit and canard they have picked up during the day. If the husband meekly suggests that all this need not be true, they feel cheated and outraged.

Wives also convey their views about individuals, through asides and innuendoes. The talk is about Mansingh. Suddenly, the wife interjects, "I don't think he is sufficiently respectful towards you. He did not call on us when your grandmother died." Or, "Don't trust Vajralingam. I don't like his face."

Personal staff is an enormously fecund source of speculation. Whether you like it or not, your PA, peon, driver, orderly, cook, everyone of them watches you constantly. In the car, you let yourself go with unabashed frankness, oblivious of the wide open ears of the man at the wheel. At the dinner table, you flirt with a colleague's wife *sotto voce*, but you are not inaudible to the bearer standing so impassive behind you. Your smile, your frown, accessibility, standoffishness, intimacy, coolness—every gesture and word is noted and reported.

Then you have the newsmen, their long noses hyperactive in smelling out any incident with *the* mildest malodour. They pass through the corridors of power, wearing a deceptively bland expression but with the olfactory nerve agog. They take surreptitious peeks at open files and eavesdrop with seeming disinterest on official chatter. Every blessed Minister is bursting with leaks. There are only two catches: the source cannot be disclosed, and you get the version favourable to the leaking Minister. But this is easily remedied by obtaining the account of the person leaked against. By the afternoon so many renditions of the same story have been heard that it is not difficult to distinguish the dissembling from the fact. Some scribes also act as latter day Narads, provoking feuds among members of the Cabinet in order to reap a harvest of headlines.

The bazar is an omnibus term for the drapers, butchers, architects and so on. Many of them have a vested interest in the life and philosophy of the modern overlords. So Mrs. Khanna, the svelte socialite wife of the man who supplies stationery to the Secretariat does not commit the gaffe of serving sugared tea to the diabetic director. There is pooling of information, by the hotelier who reports a visit by Ram Babu along with a female of dubious virtue to the Honeymoon Suite, the bank manager who has watched a huge hole develop in his saving account and the lawyer who drafted the reply to her notice asking for exemplary damages. The story becomes well-rounded, complete, conclusive and is soon the talk of the town.

To conceive of diese grapevines as independent of each other would be ridiculous. They behave as vines do, tendrils outspread in circular exploratory motion, intertwining and interpenetrating. The scandal spreads like galloping cancer, from mouth to ear. Each one adds on his own little bit of *masala* or fact, prejudice emphasizing the negative, preference glossing over it. With each narration, the picture achieves verisimilitude till it attains a perfect resemblance to the real face. Relationships that appeared amorphous, curtained by the dark, are pithily illuminated as by a pencil spotlight.

The grapevine carries all kind of gossip, but this can be subdivided, for understanding, into News, Rumour and Opinion. *News* refers to hard facts, things that have happened. Like who got the job, who bagged the contract, who is on the panel. *Rumour* is news-in-the making, things that are fluid, still happening. Like who is carrying on with whom, what someone's price is and whether he is close to the top boss. *Opinion* is interpretation of news, rumours and things yet to come. Like how long the present Government would last, when X' s mistress is likely to supplant the wife, whether Z can stage a comeback despite his ambivalent stand before the Wah Commission.

There are many who are not sure how to treat the grapevine. 'Is it dependable?' they ask. In order to facilitate their task, I have tried to analyze the situation and come up with the following laws:

1st law: If a rumour is persistent, it need not be true.

Sometimes a rumour achieves persistence because of certain fortuitous factors which are given undue importance. For example, Jacob was reported to be close to the top boss. The evidence was that whenever he called on the t.b., their gup-session was an extended one. Research showed that Y called on the t.b., around the time he went for number one. Thus what was misconstrued as intimacy was nothing but constipation.

2nd law: If a rumour is denied, it is bound to be true.

In other words, never believe a rumour unless it is denied. No one bothers to contradict a canard. The truer a story is, the stronger is the language one is forced to use to dismiss it as the "figment of someone's demented imagination".

3rd law: If the rumour says someone is honest, suspend judgement. If it brands him as corrupt, believe it.

Wherever there is smoke, there is bound to be an inefficient engine around. Rumour is specific about à person's weakness. If he is a teetotaller, it does not impute dipsomania, if gay it does not link his name with women. A tough cop might be dubbed authoritarian or Hitler-like, never a milksop.

But a reputation for uprightness might have arisen because he has not been caught ... yet.

4th law: Don't believe anyone who says he got it straight from the horse's mouth.

Check with the horse. It is true that most secrets leak out in Government from the equine orifice. I remember a Chief Minister who hit the ceiling every time classified information turned into a scoop. He foamed at the mouth and threatened to suspend the officer responsible for the serious lapse. A probe revealed that CM was himself the confidential source.

I am sure no one is surprised at this disclosure. We Indians are notoriously incapable of eating a story and digesting it, letting it become a part of the blood. We are glib, gushy, garrulous, ready to share private communications, domestic confidences and State secrets with any man in the street. As soon as we have shoved the trunk under the seat and loosened the tie, the fellow travellers on a rail journey become our bosom friends, fit to receive all kinds of inputs, from autobiographical reminiscence to unpriced advice. No bribe is needed, except a receptive ear and a respectful demeanour. If Bond ever came to India on Her Majesty's service, I am sure Dr No would buttonhole him on the Deccan Queen and reveal all about Goldfinger's smuggling racket. His double-O prefix would just be the silence so still.

People also divulge secrets because it makes them feel important to hold offices so high that they are trusted with classified information. If they could not show off, it would not be worthwhile being in those positions.

Some disclose secrets on the cynical ground that you would come to know anyway, from some other source.

There are others who are in the information game and believe that people tell secrets to those who tell them secrets.

And so the game goes on. And with it the grapevine tendrils keep curling and unfurling forward.

But there is the odd man out, like old, weather-beaten Mr Quereshi, frigid, taciturn, a bottle with a stuck-down cork. To him, one day, entered Agnani and the following conversation took place:

Q. Have my posting orders been issued, Sir?

A. Have they? Perhaps not.

A. You are not sure, Sir?

Q. I am not sure. I will have to check.

A. May I know where I am likely to be posted?

Q. Has the proposal been received? I do not remember.

A. (*tired of the game*) Here is the order, Sir.

Q. (*unfazed*) Oh, the orders have been issued already, have they?

A. Yes, Sir. They bear your signatures.

Q. (*looking*) Are these my signatures? (*reluctantly*) Yes, perhaps you are right …

Mr Quereshi retired in 1978. They don't make them like that any more.

17

Sa'ab Gusal Mein Hain

A few rare persons let the phone ring once, lift it smartly and say, "Tiwari here …" or words to that effect.

Most people are inclined to dodge the phone. And they have solid gounds for this propensity. Take the case of this fellow who says he was in college with you. He has not the haziest resemblance to anyone you knew. You exert yourself, put black hair back on a bare scalp, make the dark pouches disappear, erase the wrinkles and at long last he seems to have a tolerable likeness to a boy you faintly remember. And this obscure, half-forgotten blur on your memory disc has the cheek to insinuate that lowest tenders are not accepted in Government, that selections do not take place on merit. And he wants you to intervene. All because you had the ill luck to go to college contemporaneously with him.

So what do you do when he calls you up? You cannot ask him to buzz off, for then he will broadcast to all who care to listen, "That so-and-so! Just because he is in the IAS he thinks he is someone great. You know what he told me when I asked him for a small favour: that I should not worry because every decision in his department is taken on merits, (*sneeringly*) as if one did not know …"

The self-repecting officer tells his PA to *tarkao* the rascal, or at least to *talofy* him.

And the PA, that heaven-sent intermediary between you and the big bad world, that bluffing buffer, that comforting angel who wards off all Satanic attempts to entangle you in mundane matters, tells the caller, oh! so sweetly "Sorry, sir, Sa'ab is in a meeting."

And when this idiot calls again, you have gone off to another meeting. And another meeting. And yet another meeting. Till it appears to the persistent caller that you are never in the office and life is for you an interminable succession of meetings.

I once had a PA who objected to this fending off on moral grounds. "But sir," he contended, "How can I say you are in a meeting when you are not in a meeting?"

I squelched the question and resolved his moral dilemma with a counter plea that everything in life was a meeting. One was always meeting people at conferences, on tour, in one's office. So even if I spoke casually about the weather to someone in the corridor, it could be construed as a meeting. And when I was doing files, it was a meeting of minds, albeit on paper.

The problem is really grave when it comes to answering the residential phone. In golden times, the benign government sanctioned you a telephone orderly. This hoodlum was a veteran of myriad verbal jousts; he had a tamed mind, a supple conscience and a tongue honed to perfection.

But as so ugly often happens in bureauracy, people tend to become too similar in their reactions. The Chief Secretary of a large State had the infernal habit of ringing up his district magistrates every day. Imagine his consternation when in district after district across the State he was told by these sure-footed major domos: "*Sa' ab gusal mein hain*." This was the one answer he got at 5 a.m., 4 p.m. or midnight. The Sa'abs were eternally in their bathtubs.

This led to the celebrated circular which exhorted district magistrates to either desist from ablutions or designate a specific half-hour for them.

But an edict is no cure for a basic malady. The flunkeys now varied their litany to say that Sa'ab had gone for a walk, a swim, or that he was at prayers or having breakfast.

So the Chief Secretary removed the telephone orderlies from the scene. I wonder if he can speak to his DMs now.

One thing is clear. The absence of people trained to ward off telephone friends is felt by all. More than anything else, there are the hazards associated with entrusting this vital chore to the uninitiated.

I recall a servant who could never ever get the order of questions right. I told him he should approach the devil in three easy steps. First, ask who was speaking. Second say that he would see. Third, after an interval, declare that Sa'ab was not there.

When he got his first call, the shrewd chap at the other end asked him whether I was in. "Yes," said my servant, and added a belated, "Who is speaking?" After the damage had been done, he said he would see whether Sa'ab was at home.

Perhaps it was Sunder Lai who informed a caller, "Sa'ab has asked me to tell you that he is not at home." I am not exaggerating. Come with me to Shimla and I will show you this pious soul who always adhered to the truth, as his mom had advised him to do 20 years ago when he left his village for sin-filled climes.

I find it easier to train the wife and children in these devious ways. Their IQ is higher, so there are no egregious blunders. When I mooted the idea for the first time, my son objected. But when I pointed out how critical the straight-faced telling of lies would be for any career he might choose to adopt, he agreed that it was never too early to start. Now he is a black belt in call camouflage.

The entire gambit depends on this "Please hold on, I will see" business. God alone knows if the callers do catch on. Perhaps they imagine a huge rambling mansion, in one corner of which rests the phone, while the master of the house could be anywhere—poring over learned tomes in the library, improving his marksmanship in the shooting gallery, practising putts on the mini-golf course or taking a stroll through the acres of lawns attached to his castle.

Probably, we fool no one. The other day, I found a friend eyeing my prominent paunch with some interest. His comment: "When-ever I ring you up, your servant says you have gone out for a walk. Well! I must say your walks do not seem to do you much good."

Whether effective or not, one has to play the game. And the trickiest part comes when you are alone at home. There are no buffers now. The chips are down; you are face to face with reality. The phone rings. What do you do?

I am not sure how others react to this situation. I for one have perfected a servant voice, somewhat nasal, a wee bit overpitched. After every sentence I say, "*Hainji*?"

as if I am a little deaf. There is a rural bias to the pronunciation. I pretend not to understand English. Then, if it is someone I want to talk to, I switch on my own voice; but if I don't I tell him I am not in.

Recently, a particularly obnoxious vixen said to me, "It sounds fantastic, but your servant's voice resembles yours quite a bit. Have you ever noticed it?"

The dear old lady had a puckish twist at the corners of her wrinkled mouth. I am not quite sure whether she was really mystified or just pulling my leg.

PART FOUR

Going Like A Bomb

18

Darbaris, Doormats, Sanyasis et al.

There is such an infinite variety of IAS officers as to make it the task of Sisyphus to document each little variation of working style. Every officer has a distinct, well-defined personality which puts its stamp on all his actions. Still one can conceive of some broad categories.

A way of thinking that is rather common may be termed as the Darbari style. This type is easily identified at the very first glance. The darbari officer is never alone and palely loitering. Go at any time of night or day; he is surrounded by his admires and hangerson. Some are his immediate subordinates who are there to minister to his tiniest wish. Others are clients of the department: they wait for such favours as he may choose to bestow when the mood is upon him. A few are non-descript *chamchas* who have nothing better to do; he does sometimes throw an odd crumb in their general direction. The ambience is that of a royal court. All fawn upon the officer with slavish grins printed on their faces. Tea is followed by coffee, cold drinks, milk-shake, fresh orange juice, betel leaves and so on, interminably, Towards dusk the venue shifts to a favourite haunt more suited to activities nocturnal.

Then you have the Kremlin style which is the bang opposite. Here the officer sits cold, austere, forbidding, formal, in a tall straight-backed chair. His room is Brobdingnagian and his diminutive form eclipsed by a gigantic table. A red light is on outside the door, where is a liveried heavyweight champion with spiky moustaches sits on a stool to prevent the ingress of the *hoi polloi*. The officer is always engaged, either in very important meetings or in disposal of most urgent files. When he condescends to grant an interview, there is a disdainful twist to his mouth. He does not invite you to take a seat. His manner shows impatience, making it plain that he has better things to do. He is brusque, sparing of words and plays his cards close to the chest. He does not consult his colleagues, he issues commands. He squeezes the last ounce of authority from the office he holds. If he grants even a provident fund advance, it is with the expectation of eternal gratitude.

An increasing proportion of officers now behave in the doormat style. They know not whom they may offend if they take a decision, so they take great precautions not to. Everyone else seems to represent a Mighty Power. The minister is the immediate boss; the MLA has direct access to CM, can cause harassment with assembly questions and grill them in Vidhan Sabha Committees; the press correspondent holds the mighty scepter of the fourth estate; the non-gazetted employee is the member of a gargantuan federation whose threat of direct action makes the government shiver in its shoes; even the technocrat, encouraged by the manner in which everyone else is gunning for the bureaucrat, bares his teeth once in a while. But the IAS officer is a tongue-tied stooge, bears all the humiliation heaped upon him without opening the perpetually sealed lips, never goes on a strike under the mistaken notion that he is a part of the establishment, and presents a weak, apologetic smile hoping to mollify everyone. He is highly insecure and gives a start at every crackle of a twig in the administrative jungle. He opens the morning newspaper with timorous trepidation, fearful that his tenure of six months is over, not knowing where he will be shunted off to next. He appends his tentative approvals on sensitive files in the manner of a high-strung soldier negotiating a minefield, not knowing when some case will explode unexpectedly in his face. He is afraid to air his views. If he agrees with what has been suggested, he is a party to the decision without knowing why. If he dissents, he can be branded as a dangerous anarchist. It seems safer to take the easy way out and mumble something unintelligible. If in the process he starts resembling a doormat and has a succession of people wipe their dirty feet all over him, he does not seem to be conscious of the indignity of the situation.

We also have the sanyasi style of functioning, when an officer exhibits withdrawal symptoms of an extreme kind. Having broken his head against some obstreperous wall, he decides to steer clear of all obstacles in future. There is about him a world-weariness, an ennui, a philosophical detachment. He stops talking in meetings, contributes nothing on files and looks appropriately blank if addressed in specific terms. Gradually he is relegated to the back-benches where he is happy to hibernate in holy aloofness. He attends office as if doing the government a special favour. He returns home with the air of one who could have as well vanished into a forest. Life is for him a sort of compulsory exile which one has to go through with spartan fortitude in the hope of a glorious hereafter.

At the other end of the spectrum is the Wajid Ali Shah type, who treats the service as a sort of extended holiday. The day he enters office he bids a hearty lifelong goodbye to his books. These were means to an end; he needs them no longer. He looks on the job as a conduit for the various pleasures that life has to offer. He accepts dinner invitations from all and sundry and insists that the choicest liquor be served. He travels to sight see and shop to foreign climes if he can. He has himself nominated to training programmes held in five-star hotels and on board luxury liners and spends his time swimming or playing golf. He openly flirts with helpless subordinates. He takes all the loans he can from government or public institutions and builds immovable property all over the place. He is always buying and selling shares. He chooses cushy postings where there is tremendous patronage and literally no work. He is particularly fond of corporations where he can entertain and be entertained with impunity. He is always on tour, because he can indulge his sundry inclinations only at a safe distance from his wife.

Let us take one more type and be done. This may be referred to as the Beast of Burden style. Such an officer is literally weighed down with the avoirdupois of office. He treats files as enemies, which he has to vanquish fast or be vanquished. No sooner does a paper land on his desk than his blood pressure leaps into the nineties. He does not rest till he has cleared it off his table. If a file remains with him overnight, his heart misses several beats for fear that he might have delayed a top priority case. Whenever an additional charge is to be assigned, he is the natural choice. He is surrounded by files, sleeps, with files and even smells of files. Long after all other lights in the Secretariat have been switched off, the lone star of his window remains a mute witness to his solitary vigil over the affairs of state.

Such an officer has just one fault. He suffers from the Indispensability Complex which is an incurable and sometimes fatal disorder of the emotions.

19
Wading Through The Muck

Whether we like it or not, the process of governance proliferates a plethora of paperwork. Letters, notes, files, telegrams, returns, sitreps, telexes, fax copies are literally showered on us like confetti at a birthday bash. If people do not sink in this sickening swamp of scribbles and scrawls, it is only because they have uncovered varied modes of survival.

A unique method, practiced by just one bureaucrat in history as far as I know, is the Sofaset style. This officer not only abolished the file but all appurtenances thereto likewise. He had no chair, no file-rack, no in or out trays, no penstand, not even a table. The spacious room had wall-to-wall carpeting, a sofaset with deep cushions and a glass-topped coffee table. Anyone seeking orders walked in casually, no papers in hand, as if paying a social call. Coffee was served by a liveried bearer resplendent in red sash and snowy glove. The problem was dissected, debated upon and disposed of. No record of the meeting was kept. The subordinate just went back to his room and issued orders.

The snag in the sofaset style was its rootedness in trust. The underling had really no defence if the numero uno declined to back him up, not even a wee little initial on a file. No wonder the style has had few takers.

The most popular method of wading through the muck and emerging unblemished may by called Don't-Open-the-String (DOS) Technique. One of the besetting sins in a curious mind is this propensity actually to want to read the preceding notes, once the tape holding the file, together has been unknotted and the flap pressed back. This leads to avoidable dissipation of precious time, which could be spent much more edifyingly on such crucial matters as mugging up the Civil List or nodding one's noggin in the durbar.

The DOS Technique involves a search for the exact place where the previous noting has ended. Sometimes, one may even have to lift the flap a bit, in order to locate the precise area where one's thumb impression should logically be affixed. This no doubt a bore, but can't be helped, as a signature wide off the mark is likely to raise eyebrows.

In case one has a strict conscience, a terrible martinet of a conscience, it would be wise to appease it by going through the motions of reading the note. Here, one could practice the Inverted Pen Methodology for expeditious results.

Once the note to be perused has been identified (and one need not bother about notes from page1, as some foolish zealots try to; just the last one will suffice), all one has to do is to hold the pen upside down and move it along the lines in rapid-fire zigzag fashion, pretending to read and even to assimilate. If the pen is held nib down, a slight negligence may cause it to strike the paper and inscribe jumbled lines on it. Fountain pen users may bestow an unintended blot, if the zigzagging is too vigorous.

The Inverted-Pen Methodology should be used in conjunction with the Assembly-Line Procedure, to achieve Iacocca-like results. The latter involves the stationing of a peon on either side of your chair. The minion on the left lifts the file, opens the string and holds it aloft. The moment there is a vacant space on your table glass, he places the file in the centre, presses back the flaps, and goes on to the next one in his pile. The peon on the right watches the inverted pen with an eagle eye. As soon as the signature is appended, he applies the blotting paper, smartly lifts the disposed of file, ties the string and lets it fall noiselessly on top of *his* pile.

Thus all the drudgery is taken out of your job and even the bidi-wiggling peons progress, albeit tardily, towards a state of fuller employment. Time and motion studies have indicated that by the simultaneous application of the twin techniques, there is a 35.7% reduction in disposal time.

A logical question will at once rear its unshapely head. What to do with the time saved? Read novels? This could be hazardous; a footloose boss may saunter in with unexpected velocity and claim your reluctant attention just at the juicy bit where the hero is about to uncover the secret of the mysterious lady in the gossamer veil. Practise putting on the CPWD carpet? The ball may lose its mind trying to decide which hole to fall into. Flirt with the coquettish Under Secretary? She may mistake your frivolous foolery as a solemn expression of honourable intent.

An easier option is to do what one of my illustrious superiors did. He learnt Spanish in the first year, German in the second, and when I was posted out he had just started on Chinese.

But suppose the note has been read. What does one do with it?

In days of yore, things were simpler. If you were an illiterate magistrate, the learned *peshkar* told you where exactly you had to sign, and more significantly, whether it was to be a full-blooded signature or an innocuous initial.

Anyone who attempts to survive today on the strength of his signing skills is bound to come a cropper. Gone are the times when you could boast of the telegraphic terseness of your prose. Witness the celebrated “Ref PUC. DFA”. Today’s bosses go for comprehensive, analytical, self-contained notes.

It will not do to say that the Desk Officer’s five page effort is a saga of unblemished officialese. Every one else is supposed to contribute too. You can use your adroitness at precis-making and pen a two-page executive summary. You may expound on the theme in 20 pages of pompous verbosity. But reiterate you must or perish!

There is a crevasse here into which it is easy to fall. Suppose you are one of those who ought to have gone into a university or a research centre, and have a pathetic predilection for penning a thesis every time a file is submitted to you. It shows you joined the wrong profession. All that your sore thumb (if you write by hand) or sore throat (if you dictate) is likely to achieve is the honorific of ‘Doctor’ behind your back. Most higher-ups will tend to go around your treatise and read the note just before, to grasp what it is all about.

I know several of these filo-philes, who do not refrain from taking their files to bed. Very often, their wives have to compete for attention with these dusty mistresses whose paper vestments rustle every time they turn. It is not uncommon for a sprightly belle to catch hold of an offending file which pokes an obtrusive corner into her back and throw it out of the window.

Another variant on the theme is sitting late at office, burning midnight mercury rods. Here you offend the personal staff, who are accustomed to the payment of overtime allowance for leaving office early and coming in late. Such officers are amazed at the quick turnover of their staff, who seem to get transferred as fast as they are posted. Soon the word gets around and then your boss wonders what the hell is wrong; no one seems willing to work with you.

The only time you can justify such conduct is when there is a lady private secretary, young and comely, who is complaisant to boot, and the so called “late-sitting” is in fact a cover for discreet escapades.

With respect to speed, there are those who cannot handle a file even for 20 minutes without ejaculating a premature note, while others consider a fornight as insufficient time for the preliminary fore-play. The former keep a clean desk, their out-tray competing frantically with the in-tray. The latter lose no sleep even if every conceivable inch of space in their room is inundated by files, reports, books, returns.

There is a Law of Inverse Speed operating here, which the speedsters never become aware of. Enunciated in layman's language, the law states as under:

"The higher the speed of disposal of files, the more files one has to dispose of every day."

A cynic, who was also a statistician, once proved conclusively at a seminar that if the speed of disposal were reduced to zero, the flow of incoming files would likewise be reduced to nought in due course. Finally, all the files in the department would rest in peace in the officer's room and the subordinates would have no further papers to process. Thus trying to solve problems fast is a mug's game.

Outsiders are not concerned with reality. If they visit Agarwal's office and find him hidden behind mountains of paper-work, they commiserate with him. If they go to Banta's office and find him blowing bubbles in the air while reading a newspaper, they go home and write a letter to the editor asking the Government to abolish his post which is so obviously a sinecure.

This is why, if you cannot help being fast in disposal, at least keep some dummy files on the table, so that if a visitor drops by, you can pretend to be busy.

20

Ape Antics in North Block

At the peak of the budget fever, someone asked P.K. Kaul, former Cabinet Secretary who had also been Finance Secretary, "Is it true that Finance Ministry officials are locked up in North Block for several days on budget duty?"

Kaul gave a serious reply as befitted an ex-senior bureaucrat speaking on national television. Had I been there, I could not have resisted the temptation of referring to the monkey population of North Block. I do not think the process of budget preparation would be complete without elaborating upon their contribution.

Imagine to yourself a Deputy Secretary of the Tax Research Unit, totally engrossed in calculations of excise duty on tiny industries or whatever. He sips uncountable cups of coffee, while cogitating on the repercussions of this rate or that. Nature decrees that sooner or later, those Yamunas of hot beverage would be converted into something he wants to rid himself of. He gets up from his chair, still muttering to himself, and proceeds towards the desired spot.

Imagine the scene. Economy instructions have ensured that all lights but one in the corridor have been switched off. Outside, it is the cold darkness of December. The Deputy Secretary ambles along, thinking of duty structures, and turns a corner.

Suddenly, he comes face to face with a large, stern, male monkey, surrounded by his considerable retinue. He is the King Monkey of North Block, holding his court in the relative warmth of the stately corridor. Is he happy to see the august proceedings disrupted so rudely by a bespectacled, mumbling, bumbling Deputy Secretary of the Tax Research Unit? You can bet your trouser buttons he is not.

He mutters, he snarls, he growls, he makes faces. He makes his royal displeasure known in no uncertain terms. And the Deputy Secretary, a veteran of 15 years' standing in Government, does not tarry to explain. He retires precipitately, some would say ignominiously, from the scene, And runs back to his Tax Research Unit. By the time he reaches there, he has forgotten why he had emerged from it in the first place.

You think his shattered nerves would formulate the tax proposals in the same manner as he would if the King Monkey had not intervened? Not by a long shot. The budget proposals are now radically different.

This may possibly be called the indirect impact of the apes of North Block on Government policy. But instances are not lacking when the monkeys take a direct paw in policy formulation.

Suppose you have applied for an exemption from excise duty on grounds that are impeccable. You have received assurances at sufficiently high levels that the proposal would be considered favorably. As the case wends its slow ponderous way from table to table, you follow its fortnightly progress with ill-concealed glee. That exemption seems to be within your grasp already.

Suddenly, one day, the file disappears without trace. The movement of the file cannot be deciphered. The registers are silent, the computers inscrutable. What could have happened? Why? With what motive? A hundred questions rear their ugly heads.

All the speculation is just a waste of time. What has happened is very, very simple. It is the good old *Deus ex machine*. Divine forces have intervened in the form of Lord Hanuman.

Once again, in this holy land of Bharat, a monkey has made history!

21

Convoking the Cretins

The immutable, unalterable fate of a civil servant, when he is not attending someone else's meeting, is to have one of his own. A poetaster once remarked that bureaucrats are always eating, meeting or cheating. He forgot to add that often all three are simultaneous. There are people whose brains reside in their stomachs: the wise man calls any such to a luncheon meeting and swindles him in the soup, cheats him with the chicken and defrauds him at the dessert.

LIE (Laser Institute of Electronics, for short) has given out that 93.7% of a higher bureaucrat's time is spent in such forgatherings of the faithful. Yet, one would scan in vain the lists of compulsory training programmes for titles like "How to Sleep in a Meeting without Snoring"; or 'How to Impress the Chairman without Having Read the Agenda'.

How is a successful meeting organized? Clearly, the primary objective is to ensure that all one's proposals go through, without the obstreperous members (OMs) trying to tilt the boat. So it is best to send notices for meetings through telegrams, time to be delivered just forty-eight hours in advance. As soon as one is sure they would have booked the air tickets, a cancellation telegram may be dispatched. This should arrive minutes before the OMs are to leave for the airport.

If the stratagem is repeated twice, one may be assured that no OM will ever show up. To keep the record straight, a letter should be sent once a year to their bosses, complaining sweetly about the OM's non-attendance of the last five consecutive meetings.

As for the agenda, this should neither be slim nor readable. The style of one of the philosophical tomes on the Bhagwad Gita can serve as a model. One line of text should be accompanied by reference to at least two footnotes, one appendix and three annexures. A minimum agenda length of two hundred fifty pages should be aimed at.

This would, of course, be the size of the circulated agenda, which in best circles is only one-fourth of the whole. The rest is foisted on the unsuspecting members in the meeting itself, on the specious ground that certain confidential documents had to be held back, that the report of a committee was received the previous night or that there would be contempt of the Supreme Court if a particular item was not decided that very day. The most contentious matters should naturally figure in the third supplementary agenda, which is circulated five minutes before the end of the meeting.

On how early an agenda should be sent to members, there is a violent controversy among the experts. The "One Day Two Nights" school holds that members are apt to be careless if the agenda is sent two whole nights in advance. They tend to procrastinate and put off thinking they have all the time in the world, and in most cases, end up by not reading the agenda at all. The "Night Before school", however, feels that this is too great a risk to take. They do not object to the nights so much as to the sunny day in between, when the groggiest member may take a peek at the fearsome folder.

What happens when the meeting itself takes place? It mainly depends on what has gone before. The dynamic convenor keeps a vigorous morning schedule of visit to site, where the doddering fogies trot up and down arduous slopes. This is followed by a five course lunch, with beer and gin flowing freely, and a dozen sweet dishes to match. The post-prandial meeting that follows is apt to be a quiet affair, punctuated, now and then, by a light snore from an Obstreperous Member now at peace with the world.

There are meetings and meetings: Ceremonial Meetings, at Raj Bhawans, where beribboned generals rub shoulders with bumbling bureaucrats, and social climbers sidle up to snooty celebrities for tactical snapshots. The most significant aspect of one's behaviour at these binges lies in not resting elbows on the table and not making crunchy crackles over coconut cookies.

Proforma Meetings, which are called to ensure that information, to be filled in on performae circulated in advance, is actually sent in by various departments. Enormous time is wasted in these get-togethers, and a restructuring of the basic format seems to be called for. One would advocate stationing of a bonny lassie to welcome each participant at the entrance, collect the proforma and place a rosebud in his buttonhole. This could be followed by a refreshing tea and cake, and so on to the exit with another bonny lassie handing out "paans" for the road.

Action Meetings, say for a VVIP visit, is where all the participants know in advance what they have to do. The convenor has already circulated the duties of each official, and the meeting is held in order to be reassured that they have read the circular. If he could peruse their minds as they sit the meeting out, he would hold one more meeting to feel confident that they had actually heard what he said.

Then the decision meetings, becoming rarer and rarer, like some vanishing bird species, as the decision tends to be deferred till a more propitious moment, or till it is taken for you by a crisis situation. The alibis for postponement are numerous—more facts are needed, the law is not clear, the position in other states is to be ascertained, the mind of the boss is to be read. The easiest solution, which does not look like inaction, is to appoint a sub-committee.

When on the way to attend a meeting, one should go with open eyes lest one collides with an obstrusive piece of furniture or loses one's footing and falls downstairs. But once in, the best formula is to enter into a cataleptic trance, with eyes open and mind shut. Meeting-time pastimes are numberless. One can doodle one's subconscious on to a writing pad. Catch up on one's mail. Improve one's mind with a book or magazine. Take a snooze. Write poetry. Recite a mental mantram. Pick one's nose. Daydream. Have whispered conferences with the adjacent member. Do anything, except attend to the business at hand.

But one should never be caught napping. Suddenly, the chairman might call one's name and pop a question. It is at such critical moments that one's *sang-froid* is tested. A novice may stutter and stammer and fumble and make a fool of himself. A veteran would rise to the occasion, with a riposte that seems to mean quite a mouthful.

Let us take the following reply as a sample:

"Mr. Chairman, you have raised a fundamental issue, a very significant issue, which has, if I may say so, grave consequences for all of us. Let me say first of all how grateful I am to you for giving me this opportunity to present my views before this august forum. I cannot say that what I am saying now represents the final word on the subject. But I can state without fear of contradiction that ..." etc. etc.

A senior colleague once told me how he had delivered lectures on yoga to foreign audiences, while he himself had scant knowledge of the intricacies of *asanas*. Whenever he was cornered by an overinquisitive Yankee, he would look at the curtains and say, "This yellow chintz goes well with the sepia wall." And his audience would shout "Zen method, Zen method" and clap the questioner shut. This colleague had to make a rather ignominious exit from service. I am not sure, therefore, whether the Zen method is really worth trying out on Chairmen of meetings.

As to one's stance vis-a-vis other members, it never does to be overly critical, for this might boomerang. Nor is a milksop considered brilliant. Therefore, let the barbed sallies fly forth at timid adversaries, keep the mild innuendoes for the half-witted; be cravenly conciliatory to those who can hit back.

There may be occasions when one has to act as Chairman. This is the time to forget that the Chairman, like a speaker, is not supposed to talk. One should let loose on the assembled listeners the protracted story of one's life. Narrate the victories that never took place. Recount the defeats but present them as revolts, where one lost a mere battle in order to win a later war. Describe one's skirmishes with authority, as if one has ever been a glorious rebel in shining armour. Mention that famous remark made by a visiting bigshot about oneself—a remark that one is too modest to acknowledge publicly as true, but a remark made nevertheless.

As Chairman, one should never commit the blunder of crying halt to the garrulous or of sweetly persuading the silent sams to unburden their chimerical souls. Nor is it feasible to compel strict adherence to an agenda that no one has read and no one is interested in anyhow. Let the argument be conducted in terms of Samuel Johnson's definition of the essay—a loose sally of the mind.

A really successful meeting is one for which the convenor has drafted the minutes in advance. The only changes required are in the list of participants. No one need fear that there would be voluble protests from members. For, just as the agenda is never read, so never are the minutes.

22
How To Sleep Without Snoring

All of us have oft and anon, faced the problem of how to counter post-lunch drowsiness. We have had a feast and have topped everything else (against informed medical advice) with *rasmalai*, *gulabjamun* and *kulfi* with *faluda*. Paan in mouth, we are now seated, open note-book before us, in an uncomfortable straight-backed cane chair, supposedly listening with rapt attention to a boring lecture on Sensitivity Analysis or what have you.

How the heck to keep awake? The bald lecturer with the horn-rimmed spectacles perched on bulbous nose is rambling on and on is sing-song tones that are lullabyish in effect. Our eyes widen in an effort to stay alert, we yawn surreptitiously through the nose, we nod, first gently, then jerkily, and soon enough are dead to the world.

What if, horror of horrors, as the dreary lecturer delivers his juiciest peroration, a pregnant pause should be perforated by one of our loudest snores?

To digress just a wee bit, I have often wondered why the ancient Hindus who had researched the states of mind like no else had did not talk of the fifth state — beyond the waking, dreaming, sleeping and meditative minds.

As if in answer to my prayers, recently I came across an ancient manuscript written on bhojpatras, which speaks of the *turiya-atita* mind (beyond the fourth state). Whereas in the turiya state the eyes are closed and the mind awake, in *turiya atita* the eyes are open and the mind sleeps. This is the highest state to which only the adepts can aspire, after a trillion lives of constant meditation.

For lesser mortals like you and me, I have put together simpler recipes.

The cardinal principle is: If you want a quiet snooze, never never sit in the front row. The best results are obtained in the corner seat of the last row, especially if you keep a Sikh with outsized turban interfering with the line of sight.

If you cannot sleep with your eyes open, as most of us can't put on the darkest sunglasses money can buy and have a peacable shut-eye behind their protective curtain.

For God's sake, don't nod, whether softly or jerkily or anyhow. Learn to sleep with your head held steadily in place. If necessary, grow two extra chins to prevent the forward movement. In extreme cases, you may wear a collar such as those afflicted with spondylitis do.

Above all, never, never snore. Your somnolence should be silent. No sonic booms. No sawing of wood. Not even a z-z-z.

And for inveterate thunderers, I would prescribe the American method. Put two large pieces of chewing gum, the stickiest you can find in your mouth. Chomp, chomp, chomp till your molars get stuck, and let them remain stuck.

If nothing else, at least you will not commit the faux pas of snoring with your mouth wide open!

23

How To Look A Nitwit and Influence People

I had just joined the Service when I first encountered Kang and, like the numskull I was, judged him to be a fool. He would smile at the wrong moment and say things which appeared irrelevant. If rebuffed, he never defended himself directly, but at some apt instant, sensing the relaxed mood of the boss, casually lauded his own exploits. Faced with an explosive situation, he manfully resisted the temptation of rushing to the spot and rather busied himself in a thousand other trifles. He never said no to asinine superior orders, but somehow refrained from compliance while displaying an outwardly obedient manner.

It was soon evident to me that Kang was not the nincompoop he seemed to be. It was an affectation. Since than, I have come across a host of Kangs in the service, all absurd halfwits but supremely successful. Naturally, there is a sprouting suspicion in my mind that there must be some preponderant advantage in playing the fool.

If one may draw on analogy from the animal world, protective camouflage seems to be a major consideration. The average Intelligence Quotient in the Service is not inordinately high. Nor do the exalted jobs require anything but the meanest perspicuity. Any visible symptom of extra grey matter must necessarily ring alarm bells all along the route. The C-grade intellects would find themselves threatened, their very livelihood at stake. That this is so is proved by the taunting remarks anyone doing anything out of the ordinary has to hear from his humdrum colleagues.

Then there is a certain rat-race in the Service, whatever one may say for public consumption. There is very little room at the top and people get ruthlessly axed at every step. This process is often helped along by one's own colleagues, who are the only competitors. It is easy to say to the boss, "Oh, *him*! A super-efficient officer, Sir, but you know … not particularly sound. Do you know that he writes *poetry*?" Or "An extremely good choice, Sir, but perhaps you are aware of his dipsomaniac tendencies …" . Or again "He is definitely a dynamic personality, Sir, but you have seen how he bids at bridge. Don't you feel he is inclined to be a *bit* rash …?"

Such 'good, but' type of remarks are highly effective in the subtle demolition of rivals, but no one wastes ammunition on a person who, in his estimation, is not likely to be even considered. It is here that the fool scores. Often, the non-fools destroy each other through pyrrhic warfare, leaving the field open for the non-combative fool who was never seen as a competitor.

Sometimes, when the scramble for a high-flying job is fierce, the backers of the top seeds prefer to have the chair-occupied by a boob, rather than the hated rival. The fool thus emerges a compromise candidate and is seen as a no-threat nonentity. It is another matter that he soon gives evidence of a native shrewdness and a frightening dexterity in retaining his limpet-like attachment to the chair.

Thus the fool is somewhat like a guerrilla fighter, an invisible enemy, who chooses his ground and vanquishes a superior strength through subterfuge. When he emerges from the bush, he leaves his competitors open-mouthed with dismay. All they can do at that belated stage is to be sure they do not swallow a fly.

No wonder the garrulous Gratiano declaims, "Let me play the fool'. With such high premium on seeming dimwittedness, one would expect the market to be flooded with a hundred volumes bearing titles like "How to Look a Nitwit and Influence People" or "The Encyclopaedia of Idiocy". Actually, most manuals set us on a contrary course and provoke us to look dangerously cleverer than we are. Such books ought to be shunned like Aids.

How to cogently simulate a simpleton? First, the face. People misjudge you mostly by the facade of your physiognomy. If one spends an hour or so every morning before the dressing table, one can in time learn to wear a perennially glazed look in the eyes, paste a fatuous smile on the lips, lift the eyebrows in quizzical fashion and generally appear stupid. A professional actor could be relied upon for a few practical tips.

Then, the clothes. People habitually deduce a man from his apparel. A fop or a dandy, with knife-edged crease and immaculate shirt-cuff is bound to be perceived as a venal mercenary. But a yokel wearing baggy trousers, rough *khadi* jacket and unruly hair is immediately diagnosed as a homespun innocent or a wooly-headed ignoramus.

Conversation-wise, one has to master the art of speaking non-sense in a style that makes it sound like sense. Memorize all the hackneyed expressions there are, the stereo-typed phrases, the outworn cliches, the inane generalities—every blessed word from which the meaning has been sucked out long ago. String these together with amorphous verbs which seem to connect them. The ideal talk is one which leaves the listener with a pleasant sense of well-being and comfort, does not strain his mental faculties too much and lulls him into somnolence with familiar non-threatening words, while leaving not a trace of concrete, specific ideas.

If spoken to, one should deliberately misunderstand what is being said, with an uncomprehending glassiness of expression. The open mouth, the hanging jaw, the weird angle at which the bean in held askew—everything will then combine to create a vivid picture of a man who is not all there.

The supreme achievement is a presence that is more of an absence. This is exemplified by an apparent non-participation in the decision-making process. Such people never talk in meetings and if on rare occasion they do open their mouths, it is only to suggest that the window be closed or the airconditioner switched on. They occupy the most sought after jobs, for the sake of which they had to beg, grovel and demean themselves. Yet their official version to (which you are at liberty to take with a kilo of salt) is that they never wanted to be where they are. One day, as they were quietly seated in their offices, the telephone rang and transmitted the glad news. They are still mystified as to how it happened. Perhaps, there is after all a divinity that shapes our ends.

Nor do they exercise any power! No one consults them, least of all the big boss. Have they constituted a caucus? No, Sir, no. A kitchen cabinet? Not by a long shot. They confess to you in conspiratorial whisper that they, in fact, do not *like* power. It gives them the creeps.

This persona of bumpkinhood is an assumed one. Their subtle exercise of power lies in the twitch on an eyebrow, a pursing of the lips, a gleam in the eyes, an imperceptible nod or shake of the head. If a proposal is to be approved, they carry the file in the armpit and present it for the boss' approval when his mood is right or when he is in a hurry. If it is to be rejected, they suggest that it be sent to Mr N.N.K.N. (*Nahi Nahin Kabhi Nahin*) Nair, the eternally negative bogeyman in the finance-or-law wilderness, in whose vulturelike clutches no proposal has ever been known to possibly survive.

24
Search For A Scapegoat

If the prime ambition of an IAS officer is to do the least imaginable work without actually being sacked, then he must be an ace practitioner of the art of passing the buck.

There was a colleague whose inaugural response, sight unseen, to any paper alighting on his desk was: “This does not concern me.” He would hit a blind sixer, and ever and anon the ball was lost irretrievably in the stands.

This is not a freak formula. Often, when you receive a reminder about something exceedingly exigent, you summon the case to find that the entire office has been playing musical chairs with the earlier letter for the last twelve months. Every nook and margin is tenanted with “Does not pertain to me” scrawls.

As a callow youth, I was trained by the redoubtable Buch. I still remember the advice he gave me on how “to avoid an unpleasant paper. Like any *sutra* of wisdom it was succinct: “Tear it off.”

“But, but …”, I stuttered.

“Yes think you will be caught? Not a chance. Let me tell you my experience. In 94.3 per cent cases, you will not see the face of that paper in a hurry. If there is a reminder, do not hesitate; tear it off too. In 99.8 per cent cases you shall not receive a second one. And if you do, ask for the original reference. Thou wilt never hear from them again.”

Being pusillanimous by nature, I tried just once. Believe me you, it worked!

In every office, there is a hen or two, who sits on papers and lays eggs on them. At transfer time 1500 files are recovered from their almirahs. One sureshot method of evading a decision is to refer an embarrassing paper or file to the local egg-layer.

All those dealing with personnel matters to please note. Every office may have a Modi-Xerox machine or not, but must possess its very own egg-layer.

This apart, we all have access to the traditional departments of law, finance and personnel, to whom anything can be referred for advice. They can be depended upon for any degree of delay upto six months. Their first ploy: 'File returned, it need not have been referred to us.' Second time around: 'Before we examine the case, please tell us what the case is about and what you need advice upon.' Third time: 'We have nothing to say. Administrative department may decide at their level.' In these offices, a file is disposed of only if someone approaches personally, about a dozen times. Their motto: 'If you can forget about a file, so can we."

Some tyros may consider the six months wasted. This is a juvenile reaction. In bureaucracy, it is often desirable to stay in Square One, while appearing to be constantly in motion.

The need for decision avoidance has been with us for centuries. No wonder than that different systems have been evolved to achieve the common objective. A time tested technique is to ask the fellow who has put up the case to speak. So far so good. But then one has to ensure that he is not able to. If he tries to come and discuss the matter, he can be fended off by saying that there seems to be no hurry and it can wait. When he comes the second time, he could be given a sharp, piercing look and a casual remark made that someone could infer he was 'interested' in a decision. This should hold him for a while.

Another possible line of conduct is to call for a self-contained note. This is a ploy intended to intimidate that mettlesome warrior called the Dealing Hand. Oftentimes, he tries to palm off a half-baked cryptic brief where more is assumed than stated. By forcing him to produce a complete thesis replete with policy, precedent and procedure, you ensure a desirable delay.

A classic case was one where is a lady officer asked for a self-contained note. It was put up in a jiffy. Not knowing what to do with it, she kept the file for a fortnight' and then called for a *detailed* self-contained note, hoping to browbeat the office into procrastination. Unfazed, the Dealing hand produced an instantaneous treatise. This would not do at all. So this time she sent it down once more, saying that it was too exhaustive; what she wanted was a *compact* but detailed, self-contained note. The story does not unfold what happened thereafter.

The merit of this method is that it normally takes about three months to draft a really self-contained note. If the average tenure of an IAS officer on any post be taken on actuarial basis as six months, just two self-contained notes should see him through.

Despite all the precautions, sometimes one is compelled to acknowledge that a paper falls in one's jurisdiction. One has called for all the varieties of notes one can conceive of and these have come up in a trice. The 'please speak' strategy has exhausted itself. The file has done the rounds of all the possible egg-layers and now a decision is to be taken.

What is to be *done*?

The primary premise to keep in mind is that a decision taken is a risk undertaken. Some day, at some stage, somehow, that decision may prove to be wrong. Then one is doomed.

Therefore, if decision avoidance is difficult, one should at least attempt responsibility evasion. The decision be taken in a way it can never be traced back to you.

The most popular method is that of appointing a committee. A committee is not a person; it is a neuter gender and a common noun. You cannot hang a committee, nor suspend it. Even if an infamous finding is handed down, you can do nothing except lump it.

The committee is also a dependable instrument of decision postponement. It can formulate questionnaires, appoint consultants, order surveys, engage in study tours, and when all else fails, split into sub-committees.

And there is no need to panic when in the fullness of time the committee submits its report. For that is the right time to appoint an Inter-Ministerial Committee to examine the recommendations. If the need to delay is critical, this should be an Empowered Committee of nine Secretaries to the Government of India. It is easier for the *navagrihas* to be in the identical constellation than for nine Secretaries to find a *mahurat* to foregather.

In routine matters, the safest course is just to append a signature on the file. If the decision turns out to be foolish, one can always pin the blame on the fellow who put up the case—"It must have just slipped through in the rush of work. One cannot look at each little case with a magnifying glass. What can you do if even trusted people let you down?"

Never should one commit the blunder of putting down anything on a file except the signature. One can be held accountable for even one full sentence like the innocuous 'I agree'. It might be interpreted to demonstrate one had time to think. Remember the mathematical formulation that responsibility is directly proportional to the size of one's written contribution to a file.

The signature itself should be as minuscule as propriety permits. Later, it could perhaps even be disclaimed: "You really think that is my signature? It seems more like a stain or a blot. As if a fly with inky feet had landed here for a moment."

Sometimes you may run against a churlish subordinate who tries to counter this strategy by suggesting two alternatives and daring you to choose. One need not be overawed by such tactics. The file should be sent back with a firm, terse command: "Please assess the options and resubmit with you clear-cut views."

Another well-worn method of responsibility evasion is to send the case upstairs. That is if you are not on the top floor yourself. When the crunch comes, you could possibly blame the boss or at least threaten to involve him too. If he is apprehensive about his own skin, he might in the process save yours.

If you are lucky, you may have a Natural Scapegoat working under you. If you don't try to get one posted. Then for the odd sensitive case, ask him to speak. When he has spoken, say: "As discussed." Nothing more.

Here is where you score. The Natural Scapegoat is a very trusting, gullible kind of a guy. He does not realize that by issuing orders as per verbal discussion (which you can always disown) he has put his neck in a noose.

But that is what a Natural Scapegoat is for, isn't he?

25

Baedeker In Hand

Travel, it is said, expands the mind. The wise man, eager to acquire breadth of vision, length of purse and height of finesse peregrinates far and near, with flippant frequency.

One Maniswamy broke all roving records by vanishing for an average of 29 days in a month. Having tried other recipes for moderating his behaviour, his boss finally descended to sarcasm: "Will Shri Maniswamy please discuss this case with me on his next visit to headquarters?"

Such inveterate itinerants are actuated by a variety of motives. Hoda once confided in me that his Missus was a strict vegetarian ("can't stand even the aroma of a poached egg, you know"), while his flunkies in the field never failed to serve his favourite dish—"chicken mughali" fried in pure *ghee*. Another colleague remarked that the solitary dry fruit he got at home was roasted groundnut, but he could indulge his weakness for frizzled cashewnut when out rambling.

Acting guardian to an unaffordable private car provides another strong motivation. I know of several friends who fix inspections of officers at moderate distance so as to recharge the batteries of otherwise quiescent Marutis. One trip a month suffices to subsidize the loan installment and leave a bit over for Classic cigarettes.

Many marriages have survived thus far because the husbands remain mostly on tour. Absence may not make the heart grow fonder, yet the propensity to throw the butterdish at a balding pate across the breakfast table is said to be noticeably diminished.

Then there are the Casanovas, who have a mistress at every port. They find the relative anonymity of remote resthouses and unobtrusive model quite convenient. And when the woman-eaters grow senile and lose fangs, they depend on the jackals to bring in the daily kill.

So much for inland travel. The real juice is in excursions to external climes, where all things from throat-wetter to bed-warmer are "phoren".

The Indian Civil Service had a built-in device for assuaging this appetite. ICS officers were sent to Europe for "finishing", much like the wealthy debutantes of 19th century England. By the time we invented the IAS, all that the country could afford was a measly Bharat Darshan. And lately even this has been whittled down to a quick sojourn of a few high spots in one of the native regions.

There is a helluva snob values in worldwide voyaging. Imagine two batchmates meeting at a silver jubilee reunion. Alexander, handling the Fund-Bank desk in Economic Affairs, sleek in his Gucci shoes, faintly redolent of a French cologne and pack of Dunhill in hand, looks down his patrician nose at his shabbily dressed country cousin Babu in Kolhapuris who looks after land reforms in the Ministry of Rural Development and exudes an effluvium mildly reminiscent of cowdung. Babu whispers about his visit to a remote village in Jagjitnagar block, while Alexander talks in blasé jet-lag tones of Washington and London. Within two minutes, they realize the interstellar distances between them and move apart.

For the wife; it is infinitely worse. In kitty parties, Mrs Alexander, resplendent in imported chiffon, casually mentions the laser disc player or microwave she has recently procured from abroad. Everyone gapes at her, starry-eyed and envious. Smt Babu, coarsely clad in diffident khaddar, may muster the courage to mention the bottle of pure brown honey her husband brought back from his last village tour, but finds no listeners and is consequently in the dog-house.

With the stakes so high, no wonder the clever ones have invented several stratagems for gadding about the globe. The common element in all such methods is ruthless single-mindedness of purpose.

One of the simplest methods of going abroad, if one does not mind Nepal or Hong Kong, is to have oneself nominated to those glorious training courses, for which the

National Productivity Council has justly earned a name. The programmes are run in the quiet interiors of exorbitant hotels located at tourist spots or on board luxury liners. As a bonus, one can take the spouse along, if this is to be treated as a bonus.

I remember Saxena who perambulated the planet half a dozen times with singular nonchalance. As soon as he was posted to a new job, he endeavoured to smell out the peripatetic possibilities it offered. On one occasion, he went on a study tour to explore the general prospects of technical collaboration on any project in any country. Another time, he wanted to explore how other nations had resolved their packaging problems. He visited a prominent industrial conglomerate to make an on-the-spot study of a plant manufacturing a product, ten items of which Rs 90,000 he was proposing to buy. Once, his excursion was in order to buy pulses from three continents: he feared (although there was little cause to generate that fear) that a shortage was about to hit the country. He rambled across the dark continent, trying to locate a foreign buyer who had defaulted on a payment of Rs 1.5 lakh 10 years ago.

His strategy for having a tour approved was brilliantly simple. He always went as part of a team, never alone. First, he tackled his immediate boss and persuaded him to go. Then he went to the top man and requested him to go. Then he went to the top man and requested him to be the deputy leader. Finally, he met the Minister who was happy to lead the term. After that, it was laughably easy for the Minister to take the note personally (using the armpit method) to the Chief Minister and get his okay in a weak moment.

Another key element in the tactics was secrecy. By the time people (especially those in Personnel and Finance, who could stall the move) were alerted to the possibility of another global gallivant, Saxena was back. For those he could not include in the team but whose approbation mattered, he brought trinkets—a shirt, a tie, a bottle of whisky or a cut-glass ashtray.

Talking of techniques, one cannot refrain from referring to a classic case where a blue-blooded bureaucrat, as generalist as the rest of us, got a technical paper written by a subordinate, submitted it to an international conference and then asked the Government to finance his trip, saying that the acceptance of a bureaucrat's technical paper was not only on honour for the nation, but a great tribute to the Service as well.

With such indefatigable travellers a time is bound to come when it becomes a matter of prestige to have visited every spot in the world, howsoever small or remote, it might be.

Let us say the mythical Alexander meets the legendary Saxena. Alexander casually mentions the high price of cabbage in Lesotho, a country whose very existence Saxena does not suspect. The five-second silence that follows is all the reward that Alexander seeks. He savours the glory of this moment of one man up ship, as one rolls a rare and old whisky on the tongue.

26
Croesus Consultancy

You will find any number of takers for a legitimate method of raking in millions, and no income tax please. In the IAS, there is just one route to limitless moolah—consultancy!

Imagine an impecunious officer taking a measly Rs 5,000 home every bloody mensem and ending up with an overdraft of ten thousand rupees at the end of the year. To him, like manna from heaven, drops a 30-day consultancy from a UN agency which in return for sixty pages of blah blah copied from three books, ten reports and five journals throws into his lap crisp dollar notes equivalent of a hundred thousand rupees. Will he jump through the hoop to place his grasping paws around the bonanza? You bet he will.

This mind-boggling extravagance stems an idiotic equivalence of a Harvard professor earning $90,000 a year to an indigent IAS officer drawing $5,000. That man is used to carpeted bathrooms in psychedelic tiles; this man throws a blessing God-words each time his flush works. That man gargles with champagne; this man is content to fill with someone else's imported whisky a stomach that is full of butterflies thinking of the price he will have to pay in return. In an international organization, at last, we achieve the equality between violet and red which even radical Marxists could not dream of.

The way UN organizations function can only be described as fantastic. They do not really know what needs to be done, except for the charter which defines their general objectives. So a consultant is appointed to advise what project should be taken up in each country. Then they nominate a consultant to write the project report. Another consultant examines the report and draws up an action plan. A consultant oversees implementation and a different one carries out concurrent monitoring and evaluation. A consultant then prepares the follow-up report. Lest all this hectic activity impose an intolerable strain on the harried UN civil servant, there is an obliging consultant who advises him in the tangled task of selecting other consultants.

Suppose you were to ask someone how to burst into the charmed circle of UN experts. He will feed you the official line that several sheaves of forms have to be filled in and you have got to register yourself with the FA cell of the Department of Personnel, Training, Pensions and Public Grievances and the applications are fed into a computer and a requisitions is received from a UN agency and then there might be an interview and you stand a good chance if you have the necessary expertise and experience and so on and so forth.

All this is just hot air. The UN agencies detest unknown devils even more than national agencies do, and therefore follow the venerable method of asking someone as to whether he knows someone. Fortunately, they have country-wise quotas and there are certain representatives of the various nationalities already on the campus. All the harassed UN civil servant has to do is to pick up an intercom and call the Indian he met from Natural Resources at a party the other day. "Shams," he pronounces, "Do you know any good Indian expert on environment?" Shyam, who is happy at the anglicized version of his name that calls him the humbug he has become, knows several but naturally recommends friend Raam who will soon be known as Randy Ram on the cocktail circuit.

Although they are international bureaucrats, none of the UN officials are really devoid of patriotic sentiments. So a Lebanese Director General appoints a Lebanese Assistant Director General, while a Bangladeshi Chief hires a Pakistani Training Officer he knew before the Liberation. There is a religious net, a regional net, a college net, a friendship net, and all these help in catching the fish called Subject Matter Specialist.

So entry is to be gained, by keeping one's contacts alive, unfolding the antennae, smelling out opportunities, writing letters, sending birthday cards, remembering wedding anniversaries, calling people over dinners, acting as a guide and presenting expensive gifts to all those who matter. Meeting Mrs X, an ageing World Bank bureau chief with a penchant for youthful wogs, one could invite her to Inida, take her to Goa and Khajuraho, try out some of the exotic *asansas* with her in a hotel room and send her off on a silken Kashmiri carpet. That is just by way of illustration; the method has to match the man.

You don't have to say loud why you are exuding suave solicitude for the humdrum Mrs X. She does not acknowledge it even to herself, but she knows that all the chivalrous men who roll at her feet pursue the Golconda of gold, to which she holds the key. At last, the letter arrives. You have been summoned on Author's Contract to FAO Headquarters at Rome. A report is to be written in six weeks' time. Your hotel accommodation has been booked. Your prepaid Ticket Advice has come in. What next?

A basic point one often tends to forget is that international bodies move at the pace of an abnormally slow-footed snail. IAS officers, fresh from a district where they set up tented colonies for flood victims in a trice or shoot terrorists down in imagined encounters, have a different inner programming in relation to work and time. Drafting a report is for them a task that cannot be allowed to take more than seven days, and this they can do with both hands tied behind their backs. The danger is that they many actually finish the job within a week and like Oliver Twist ask for more … work.

Old hands at the game will advise you on how to tackle the FAO. "For god's sake, don't tell them you have written the report in India itself. Don't complete the manuscript within the time allotted to you. At the end of the fifth week, have a telegram sent to yourself. Government of India wants you back at once. You are sorry but you have to leave in a hurry. Of course, you will try to return as soon as you can. You have just finished the first chapter and sketched out a rough draft for the second …"

In this manner, you achieve several goals at once. FAO understands how important you are to the Government of India. The dramatic effect is that of an over-busy filmstar who cannot tarry for a retake because the next studio has been waiting for three and a half hours already. FAO appreciates your meticulous attention to detail. You first sketch out rough drafts, then revise and re-revise till you achieve near-perfection. FAO is pleased at your pace—pedantic, scholarly, unhurried. You will return in God's own time and FAO will gladly pay the return fare.

The other counsel of wisdom is never to state that the work is over. Such a maladroit ending to a research project not only writes finis to you and your project coordinator at FAO headquarters; it also bespeaks of bureaucratic mentality supposed to be extinct in UN experts. Work can never be over. "My boy", advises the old hand, "Always talk, at the end, of the fresh challenges that lie ahead and the further studies needed to provide a reliable data base for policy formulation in the future."

As for the lady secretary allotted to you, do not commit the mistake of dictating your stuff to her. Poor dear, she is a native Roman with a scantier acquaintance of English than her Arab boss. He has not dictated to her for years. He would not know what to say, without the aid of a consultant.

The secretary will fetch you stationery and pens and library books and coffee from the vending machine round the corner and take your pages to the typing pool and photostat something from a journal and smile tiredly at your tepid flirtation.

At the end of the second day, the old hand from India will take you home for dinner, tell you how costly Rome is and over the liqueur counsel you to shift from the hotel to a pension.

If lovely lucre is your goal, as it is for most Indians, you will soon discover that a room without an attached bathroom is even cheaper, that you should gormandize on the subsidized lunch at the office and make do with a pizza and coke for dinner, that you can gang up with three other Indians in a room and assemble the breakfast yourself, that you should always go to a fast food counter and never ever to a restaurant, that 24-hour 80-channel TV in the lobby and a library book is all the entertainment you can afford, and so on.

Thus as you go along, the path is lighted up. But the million dollar question remains: can you really write a report that would be acceptable to an exalted forum like the FAO? You need not lose any sleep over this one. IAS officers may not be Subject Matter Specialists, but there is one thing that they really specialize in—the English language. There is no subject on earth the polysyllabic jargon of which cannot be picked up in 24 hours flat. The content is immaterial. Those good at gobbledygook should have a natural talent for mere manipulation of lingo.

At long last, the report is ready. And now you are in for a big surprise. You thought that the FAO chap who hired you was a nincompoop who had no expertise in anything. You were mistaken. For now he will exhibit to you the peculiar bent of his genius. With infinite patience and true courtesy, he will delicately suggest those subtle niceties which distinguish a FAO report from the garden variety. The cover, the size of margin, the headings in bold print, the para numbering, the bibliography, the index, the photographs, the maps, the entire gamut of typing technology and manuscript management.

Finally, you submit your text. After a week your coordinator arranges a conference with the inhouse expert they have. It so happens that your report was on the training system in China. They have no mastermind in training, but there is an old China campaigner. He has lost his voice, so you can listen to his mechanically magnified whisper, about how sensitive the Chinese are about allusions to Mao and the Cultural Revolution, while you nod politely and try to think of something else.

And now it is time to go home. You have collected your doubloons and as you bid your contactman *au revoir* at the airport, you remind him about the unfinished business referred to oh! so tactfully in the last paragaph …

As the aircraft heads homewards you really hope that this is just the beginning, that you will come again and yet again to El Dorado, for a month and a half every year. At this stage, it is superior even to a UN posting, for there is no disturbance either to the children's education or to your sex life.

Later, of course, if things go your way, you will think of a three-year stint, to be extended to a five-year period, so that you can earn a pension and maybe, if all goes well, retire from service and become a life-long international civil servant.

You will still be a flunkey, but what fantabulous wages!

27
Carnal Cadre

It is generally accepted that bureaucracy is a balloon already inflated beyond all decent dimensions. A little more wind and … Poof! It would burst. Wise men are unanimous that a lot of air needs to be let out so that the rest of us can breathe in comparative peace.

Yet, on the contrary side, we have this unseemly spectacle of new categories wanting to join the bandwagon. Bank employees would have us grant them pension. Municipal and panchayat staff go on strike and refuse to work, so that they are taken over as government employees and can then abstain from the grind as a matter of right. And now the practitioners of the oldest profession in the world want it to be nationalized.

The proposal seems to have been mooted after the deepest thought. Had they said bluntly that "prostitutes" be taken over, some N(o), N(ever), N(ever) Narayanan in the Ministry of Finance would have rejected the suggestion *in limine* on the ground that entertainers could never be permitted to enter the boring citadel of bumbledom. Calling themselves sex workers is a master touch.

A caviling critic might query, "Is this not a contradiction in terms? How can sex be work?" If there is anything farthest removed from work, it is sex. Workaholics rush from the hellfire of drudgery to the cool solace of a courtesan's couch. Sex is the great relaxation—the one effort that is not laborious, the one task that is not irksome, the one toil that does not tire.

But who are we to question, when the oracles who run the Non-Governmental Organizations have spoken. "Brutus says he was ambitious and Brutus is an honourable man". So if the self-righteous women who aim at the Right Livelihood Award say that sex is work, it has to be so. All that lesser mortals can do is to think out the mechanics of the transition.

And the first thing that leaps to the eye is that sex workers cannot have the ascending pay scales so fashionable among the bureaucrats. Here, it is the junior most employee who would have the youthful looks, the maximum demand, the highest price. As one becomes senior, the pay packet would shrink and keep on diminishing till it disappears altogether.

The Pay Commission would have to invent a pay scale of the following type: Rs 10,000-minus 200–8000-minus 400–4000-minus 500–0. Negative increments or decrements would be awarded at the end of each year.

Would there be only workers or officers too? This is a moot question. In the private sector, retired prostitutes become madams and run the show, using their vast past experience. On that analogy, the older sex workers would have to be promoted to the positions of District Sex officers and the like, till at the apex level you had the high-sounding Director General of Sex Operations, the oldest and ugliest hag among the lot, with a negative salary.

How would fresh blood be inducted into the cadre? It would not do to entrust the task to the Public Service Commissions, for they can at best devise competitive examinations which test a candidate's theoretical knowledge. And even in these it is the objective type test that is most in fashion. One can imagine young hopefuls scratching their ponytails, trying to work out answers to questions like these:

a) Good evening, Sir. What is your pleasure tonight?

b) Hi, handsome. What will it be?

c) Namasteji. Chai piyoge?

d) Oh, no! Not you again!!

Sex is more an art than a science. If it is the PSCs who have to choose, they might ordain the possession of a degree in science to act as a disqualification.

For a moment if we presume they can devise practical tests which check an aspirant's expertise in the art of love-making, it might be well nigh impossible to arrange the logistics of a competitive examination for a hundred thousand office-seekers across the country.

Which is why I feel that the best option might be to farm out the recruitment to private agencies, as we now place security or sanitation services on contract. This might attract MNCs like Pimp International, Trans World Touts Inc., Pan Procurer, etc., to jump into the fray and pump precious foreign exchange into our depleted coffers.

What better pump than a pimp!

28
The Crazy ACR

It sounds like SLR or the self-loading rifle. But the ACR is not a weapon, though it is used to shoot people down. For the sake of the uninitiated, let me hasten to explain that ACR stands for the annual confidential report. It is that magical document in which an IAS officer's fate is sealed once every year.

In theory, it is the sheaf of ACRs one has collected over the years which, when fed to the All-Wise Computer, puts one on the panel of Joint or Additional Secretaries, picks one up for a posting with an international organization, or cooks one's goose. Definitely not something to sneeze at!

It is, of course, a different matter that decision-making is still in the hands of human beings, who (thank the Almighty Lord!) are fallible and willing to be influenced.

There are the myopic idealists who opine that the days of the ACR are numbered. They point out that the assessment is brief, subjective, too generalized and not at all dependable.

This may be so. It is indeed so. Successive governments have constituted commissions and committees on how to replace the ACR with something else. But the ACR refuses to die. The committees' recommendations have only succeeded in making it even more cumbersome and less intelligible.

The difficulty is that the IAS does nothing concrete which you can lay your hands on. An IAS officer thinks; most of his thoughts are unprintable. He speaks; what he says is in all probability not what he means. He writes, but only what he can and should.

If objective criteria for judging his performance were to be devised, one could go totally off-tangent. How many meetings did he attend? Perhaps, a hundred thousand. Did the meetings achieve anything? One cannot be too sure. How many files did he dispose of? Certainly, many more than one would have thought possible. What was his contribution to them? It is difficult to lay one's finger on anything definite.

I have seen colleagues tearing their hair at the end of a gruelling day. Somehow, they did not have a minute to spare. They were terribly busy all the time. But what did they achieve? Frankly, they don't know. The tally seems to add to zero.

Experienced administrators know that in recording an ACR they do not really have to analyze what an officer has done. Basically, they have to describe what sort of a chap he is.

A benign government has decreed that officers be classified into five grades—poor, fair, good, very good and outstanding. Commonsense dictates that no one be awarded a 'poor' grading. If the fellow were 'poor' he would not have made it to the IAS in the first place. 'Fair' is definitely an unfair way of describing anyone. And when you are told that a 'fair' officer is considered unfit for promotion, your kind heart forbids you from awarding this pernicious grading. The 'outstanding' medal cannot be vouchsafed to all and sundry. Resultantly, the only real choice lies between 'good' and 'very good'.

Here one recalls the pious Tamil Christian who never adjudged anyone higher man 'good'. When pressed for a reason, he explained, "The Bible says God created the world and found that it was good. If what God created is good, can anything else be described as better? It would be sacrilege."

The denizens of Writers' Building, Calcutta are famed for recording adverse entries. I once buttonholed Chatto and wanted enlightenment on why half the West Bengal cadre had not made to the panel. His reply was succinct: "We did not spare even Robindro Babu. No Bengali is prepared to concede that anyone else has brains."

In Uttar Pradesh, every third officer is graded 'outstanding'. Having contributed most of the prime ministers, people of UP believe they have a divine right to rule. Overrating officers is a foolproof technique for ensuring the hegemony of UP officers at the Centre.

Recently, I conducted a Gallup poll to find out how officers decided which grading to award. The results were frightening. When they started writing an ACR, 73 per cent did not know how it would end. Only 5 per cent had decided beforehand what the grading would be. Out of these, a whopping 68 per cent based their decision on what others thought of their subordinates; only 9 per cent depended on their first-hand assessment. 97 per cent of all those interviewed confessed that they were not happy with what they had penned. Twelve per cent even wanted to recall the ACR and modify their assessment, but were not sure they would be granted permission.

On the question of supersessions, opinion is sharply divided. There are some like Mondai who as Chairman, Public Service Commission, downgrades all 'outstanding's to 'very good's on the ground that he has yet to meet a person who stands out. After a few years, all bureaucrats tend to look alike. Also, if there were a deviant by mistake, he could not have survived thus far in the bureaucratic jungle. The advantage in recognizing seniority as the sole criterion of merit is that there is no discretion which anyone can misuse; the demerit is that there is no discretion.

On the other side are those who feel that there should be ruthless weeding out of the incompetent and the merely competent. Only the best (meaning themselves) should move up. The snag here is that the best officer would generally be the one whose boss had the greatest command over language.

I know of Tsering, a tribal from the North-east, who was as parsimonious in the use of words as he was good at heart. He felt he had done his duty by a particularly brilliant officer when he wrote a gargantuan 'outstanding' across his ACR. Imagine his chagrin when he found this chap superseded by a B-grade officer whose boss had written a veritable thesis, full of hyperbole and exaggeration, on his manifold accomplishments.

Talking of the English language, one cannot but recall the tale of the semi-literate boss, who wanted to record his fulsome appreciation of a subordinate's diligence and ended up saying: "Works hardly."

29

The Admirable Administrator

Yesterday, someone told me that Karchhiwala had won the Best Bureaucrat Award. You cannot imagine what damage this little piece of news inflicted on my ego. Karchhiwala! Best Bureaucrat!! What was this world coming to?

A story that at once flashed across the mind was that of a redoubtable Managing Director of a government undertaking in the business of apple juice. Every year, with monotonous regularity, this little-known corporation used to bag an international award from Italy. The award was given away by no less a personage than the Prime Minister of Italy.

Till one day I happened to call for the file to study the phenomenon in depth. And it then instantly became clear that we were all being taken for a ride. There was an organization in Italy, which specialized in giving awards. The modus operandi was to issue letters offering such awards to various bodies across the world. All that the organization wanted in return was a measly entry fee of ten thousand dollars!

Who says we Indians are slow at picking up recipes for instant success? At least, in this area we have been quick absorbing the transfer of technology. In Delhi alone, I believe there are two thousand and thirteen such organizations. For the right price, you can now bag an award of your choice.

You may be saying to yourself—all this is okay, but what about Karchhiwala? Well, I learnt about the award at 1100 hours yesterday and at 1105 I was already on the phone, talking to Sher-chhaap Gomes, Chief of Ace Investigators Ltd.

What he has found out in the last 24 hours is incredible. It seems this organization gives fifteen awards every year. Of these, ten are genuine and these are made to true professionals, people who are really at the top of the tree. It is these names which give this award its fantastic prestige.

There are five awards which are sold. To the highest bidder. In the nicest possible way. With no compulsion. The bleeding is utterly painless.

All that happens is this. You receive a very diplomatically worded letter. It says that you have been short listed for the Best Bureaucrat Award.

P.S. Incidentally, there is a list of parties enclosed. Would it be possible for you to persuade them to give ads for a souvenir being brought out on the occasion. The total ad revenue demanded is a paltry twenty lakh rupees.

Four months later, if you show the initiative and drive so necessary for the admirable administrator, every magazine in the country will be talking about you. Well, how about it?

30
Who's On The Panel?

There was a time (they say) when entry into ICS or IAS guaranteed you a retirement as Secretary to Government of India. Promotions were automatic. Camaraderie ensured protection to weaker members of the flock. You were literally immune from transfers. To talk of suspension or arrest would have been sacrilege.

This was bad. It was the toughness, the longevity, the very inflexibility which earned us the sobriquet of the steel frame.

So an attempt was made to take away some of that rigidity. Today, the average tenure of a field officer is six months. Suspensions are a dime a dozen. Vendettas and witchhunts have resulted in arrests and detentions. And supersessions are the order of the day. An examination of one hundred backbones has revealed that not a trace of steel remains; it is all wax.

Part of the reason lies in the way promotions take place. Theoretically, for selection posts, we are supposed to gather in the best. But the entries in the confidential reports, which used to be a somewhat reliable basis for adjudging the merit of an officer, have become too erratic to serve any useful purpose.

There are some states which suffer from an excess of compassion. With peace and political stability prevailing all around, every officer manages to get an 'outstanding' entry, and none is below 'very good'.

States riven with political trouble, with governments falling like ninepins, and internal squabbles among the bureaucrats, cause untold misery to their officers. People are identified as members of particular groups owing loyally to a father figure, and their fortunes toss up and down with the luck of their mentors. The highs and lows in their ACRs refuse to be part of a secular trend.

Then there are states with a tradition of conservative understatement. An officer rating another as 'outstanding' would invite delicate frowns from his colleagues. 'It is not the done thing, old man!'—they would seem to say.

As if all this is not enough, the situation is further complicated by the comments made by politicians. A minister, who can with laborious effort just about sign his name in Urdu, suddenly breaks out into a veritable paean of praise in impeccable English. A wag then suggests that the officer reported upon must have submitted a draft for approval. A Chief Minister belatedly recalls an incident when the officer had refused to be bullied, and with blithe unconcern pens a cryptic 'At times, tends to be difficult' across the page.

Then there is emotional blackmail. I know of a conscientious boss who gave an adverse entry to a dipsomaniac, only to have the latter commit suicide a month later. The boss was shaken by the incident, but persevered. A year later, a similar entry resulted in a massive heart attck to an officer who happened to be a Brahmin. The man swore he would never pen a red entry again; he did not think much of the '*brahmahatya*' which he almost committed in the cardiac case.

Somehow, anyhow, the ACRs get written. To exude an emanation of equity. Government sets up a panel of peers who are supposed to assess you objectively and weigh you in the electronic scale for competence, courtesy and compassion. Now comes the crunch: are you going to make it to the panel or not?

What is this panel everyone seems to be talking about? No one has actually seen one with physical eyes. So one cannot swear on oath what it looks like. But I believe it is a list of names typed on a sheet of paper. Only one copy of this mythical list exists, if at all. The Cabinet Secretary is reported to have it in his personal custody. Whether he carries it in purse or briefcase, keeps it in bank locker or combination safe is one of those irksome mysteries.

While the panel is being formed, everyone keeps asking, "What happened to the panel?" "Are you on the panel?" or "Who all are on the panel?" The answers vary; no one knows. There are only unconfirmed reports based on hearsay. One person swears that the list has twenty two names on it; he has it almost from the horse's mouth. Another claims this is stale news; there was a list of 22 five days ago. Since then the scheduled caste lobby has managed to have three SCs smuggled in. Someone else says that the PM wants more tribals. A wag pipes in about the need for 30 per cent women, You have forgotten the OBCs, another pontificates with a half-mocking smirk.

In sum, there is total confusion. People whose names do not figure in the rumoured panels wear long faces. Then someone tells them they are in; they start smiling. Promptly comes a flash; they are out. Now the visages are more elongated.

God alone knows why they make a panel for Delhi. This is supposed to induct the best talent into the Central Government. Seventy-five percent of the people do not want to come to the Capital anyway. They draw higher salaries in the State, are closer to their property and relatives. They are able to secure small perks like a servant allowance, Leave Travel Concession by air, financial sanction for bypass surgery in USA, a big mansion, five orderlies, an earmarked vehicle, numberless salutes and what not. It is a Punjabi stuck in the backwaters of Kerala or a Tamilian perched on a Shillong peak who seeks a Delhi posting. You can see the same persons come again and yet again to Government of India like migratory birds. Why not have the panel for only those few who are really keen to come? At least then the percentage of those who fail to make it to the panel will not be as high as it is today.

All this is more complex than it appears on the surface. The All India Services have hitherto had one advantage over state services. If a member fell foul of the Government at the State level, he could opt for a posting in the Central Government. This was an exit route, which saved many a career from premature extinction. By keeping a very small panel, that passage is being blocked. Resultantly, the IAS will soon be as subservient as any state service.

Another reason is the overweening ambition of certain bureaucrats, who have access to the royal ears. Suppose 1961 is the year being considered for Secretaryship. The power-hungry Babu happens to belong to the 1962 batch. How to short-circuit the process? The only way is to have just a handful from 1961 on the panel, so that 1962 can also qualify for consideration almost immediately. History is witness to cases when two years were lumped together in order to achieve the same objective.

So what if one does not make it to the panel? Is that the end of the world? Not so, for then the misguided zealot who wants to serve the nation rather than just a part of it and is prepared to suffer in the cause can return to his State and live happily after. But it is also a *moonchh ka sawal*. So most people do try to get into the panel at the stage of review, by using pressure tactics, at both bureaucratic and political levels. They may not elect to come to Delhi, but they do want to retain that theoretical option and brag about it.

Promotion to the post of Chief Secretary in the State and Cabinet Secretary at the Centre is a chancy affair. Let us take the Cabsec's job. There are numerous hats in the ring. A is the senior-most, but most people discount his chances because of the testimony he gave before the Wah Commission. Next comes B. There is really nothing against him, except this relaxed, good-humoured approach to life. There are doubts as to whether he is really *sound*. C is a South Indian and the PM is not keen to have him, but this may send a wrong signal to the Southern lobby; so one cannot say for sure. D is a woman. Elevating her to this prize slot would be a very shrewd move. It would silence the PM's critics among the liberationists who have not yet forgotten his unfortunate remarks on *sati*. E has a very powerful business class behind him. While this is a clear advantage, there has been a press leak about the association and this might just about sink his boat. F is the one PM really wants to have, not only because he is also a Bengali and his wife makes fabulous *mishti-dohi* but also because he is the right man for the job.

One of them is finally selected. The seniors are sometimes left in the cold, to make ineffectual gestures, like putting in their papers. More often, they are kicked up or sideways to lucrative or high-sounding positions, to avoid unseemly controversy. Traditions among the states vary. Tamil Nadu elevates just one officer to Rs 8000; his seniors continue to hibernate at Rs 7600. In Madhya Pradesh if they make the 8th person Chief Secretary, the seven above him are all elevated to Chief Secretary's rank and status.

Over the years, certain waveless lagoons have been identified where buffetted barks can drop anchor. In the Centre we have Secretary, Official Language or Statistics, Member, Planning Commission or UPSC and the high-sounding Director General of the Council for People's Action and Advancement of Rural Technology. In States, Chairman Board of Revenue, Chairman Sales Tax Tribunal, Chairman X Project

Authority, Chairman Border Dispute Commission, Director Institute of Public Administration and the like constitute havens of refuge.

We started by saying that getting into the IAS once guaranteed you a top job towards the end of the career. Today, people are lucky if they retire as Additional Secretaries. This progressive devaluation of the service is also linked with the inroads other services have made in the corridors of me Central Secretariat. Today you scratch a Secretary, he turns out to be Ordinance Factories. You scrape off the paint from another; he is Railway Stores. And everywhere, everywhere there is the ubiquitous Central Secretariat Service which holds the Union Government in thrall.

Soon, IAS officers will go home as Deputy Secretaries. But then the service has got itself hated so much, no one will be shedding any tears over its 'undeserved' fate.

PART FIVE

A Rum Go

31

Games Bureaucrats Play

Delhi has always been the city of babus. I am sure the bureaucrats of today can trace their lineage to the venerable Vidura at the court of Dhritrashtra. The change is mainly in the tenor of the advice tendered to the king. While Vidura specialized in frank, forthright exhortations, his latter day descendants prefer the honeyed counsel so beloved of the royal ear.

What then of the much-touted differences of opinion between bureaucrats and ministers that consume so much of newsprint? Are there any babus left with the gumption needed to stand up and speak out?

I suspect not. When a bureaucrat is but a baby in the service and starts to lisp his first few words in the language called "bureaucratese", his trainers are careful in teaching him the merits of vagueness and vacuity. He can never say, "I feel". It would be too strong. It would smack of an egoistic streak in his character. He should say, "It is felt". He would perpetrate the ultimate sin if he commits himself to a course of action. "We may perhaps consider the feasibility of …" is the maximum he is permitted. When driven into a corner and if forced to take a decision, he may reluctantly agree to … well not actually decide the issue, but to set up a committee to look into the matter.

What really happens is something like this. Picture a scene in a Secretary's office. It is 7.30 p.m. Most of the Joint Secretaries have gone home to their wives and cable television. The Secretary is still in office under the mistaken notion that Secretaries do not leave office before 9.00 p.m. He has missed the lunch due to a prolonged debate in Parliament. The tepid tea and oily samosa he had instead has provoked a familiar dull pain in his stomach. He is grappling with the draft reply to Calling Attention Notice and wincing at all the errors in grammar and typing.

Enter a member of the fourth estate. The Secretary is unable to prevent his entry. Nor can he continue to peer myopically at the draft; it would not be considered polite. He asks whether the other will have coffee, praying he will refuse. The "Special" commiserates with his ulcer and agrees that the present crop of Joint Secretaries leaves much to be desired.

These words of sympathy loosen a screw in the Secretary's brain. All his pent-up emotions are released. He starts fulminating against his Minister. He overlooks the fact that he is talking to a pressman. He only sees his friend from college and feels as liberated as they did when discussing the Principal's conduct in the canteen. He forgets all he has learnt about being discreet and secretive. Some half-forgotten genetic thread from Vidura starts pulsating in his brain and, before he realized it, he has spilled the beans.

He wakes up to a sizzling story in the morning newspaper that sours the cup of tea he has started to sip. He cannot believe his eyes. That a private conversation with a childhood buddy should have crept into print amazes him. His colleagues shake their wise heads and comment that so-and-so seems to be slipping. His Minister wants him to come to his residence at 8.30 am. It is a wonder his ulcer does not burst …

The Secretary in turn is a much-execrated man. His Additional Secretary feels, perhaps not so unjustly, that he is being sidelined. He has been allotted the miscellaneous subjects of general administration, official language and coordination. Sometimes he is sent post-haste to attend meetings in the Cabinet Secretariat, which take hours and decide inconsequentials.

The joint secretaries resent the fact that have to do all the dirty work and hibernate at home, while the boss quietly goes to all the hot spots in the world to read out speeches they have drafted.

The Heads of Department are sore that he seems to have shrewdly picked up all their jargon and buzzwords, and is now able to hurl these effectively back at them in review meetings. They dream of the day they can throw off the yoke and preside over the destinies of the department in their own right.

His personal staff does not exactly love him, for he is irritable at the best of times and can cross the limits of irascibility when the ulcer throbs. They rue the day they got posted with him, hoping he would be like his predecessor, go home at 6.00 p.m. and sign all the overtime bills like a good boy.

As for his family, the less said the better. His wife has written him off as far as evening tea goes, but when he rings up at the last minute to say he is going out for dinner with a visiting delegation and they need not sit up, she wants to do some unmentionable things—both to him and herself. His offspring have decided in early infancy that the mad topsy-tursy world of the civil service is not for them. They sometimes see their father's face on Sunday mornings. It is not a very pleasant sight.

Is it that bad, you may well ask? Does he not at least boast of a friend, one friend, someone he grew up with, whom he can depend on?

Unfortunately, Delhi is most certainly not a city of friendships. Everyone here is on the make. You meet someone at a party. He is pleasant. You have a beer together, laugh a bit, munch a few savouries, lampoon the mighty and have a good time. The nice-looking stranger presents his card when you are leaving and in a moment of weakness you part with yours. It is the next day when you pick the card out of your pocket to throw it away that you realize who you have been talking to. You did not know who he was, but he knew. He leeched on to you, not accidentally as it appeared, but as part of a business strategy. In fact, he had wangled an invitation to the party. Just to be able to corner you.

Then begins a merry game. He rings up to invite you out for dinner. You try to avoid him, but as the calls continue to come with sickening frequency, you feel more and more like a fly being pursued by a spider. Until you finally tell your personal staff and the family that they are not to connect you to Mr Taneja. So you are in a meeting, or just gone out for a walk, or in the bathroom, or doing pooja or, sometimes in a mood of great daring, gone out on tour for two weeks.

At long last, Taneja gets the message and his phone calls start tapering off and one day cease. But the war of nerves has taken its toll. The children, with their innate predilection for absolute truth, start chafing at the bit and refuse to feed lies on the telephone. And it is you who feel like a pusillanimous prevaricator, who does not have the moral courage to pick up the phone himself and tell Taneja to F O.

Of course, all bureaucrats are not interested in evading the Tanejas or Tinaikars of the business world. Many of them are keen to be posted to the Ministries of Industries, Commerce or Finance, mainly in order to be the prime targets of these sharks. They have to use an elaborate gameplan to foil the attempts of the dreaded Establishment Officer to post them to the arid regions of the Minorities Commission or the Department of Programme Implementation.

The E O, as this bug-bear is affectionately referred to by his victims, is a sadist par excellence. He specializes in summoning reluctant deputationists from the states or sending back eager deputationists to the state at the most ill-chosen moments. One of his favourite pastimes is to send the name of an ambitious officer, who has sounded out the Minister of Industrial Development through his influential father-in-law, to the Department of Offical Language. But the officer is more than a match for the E O. He now sends his father-in-law to the Home Minister, to ensure that his name is not picked up in the Department of Official Language! Unfazed, the E O now pushes his name for the Department of Ocean Development. He talks to the Secretary and lists the case before the Civil Services Board the same week. The officer is picked up and his name goes for approval to the Appointments Committee of the Cabinet.

But the E O has not taken the officer's father-in-law in the reckoning. This indefatigable relative is now able to convince the State Chief Minister that he would be totally unable to relieve this particular officer at such a crucial juncture. The State administration would collapse without him. Thus the name is withdrawn from the offer list "in public interest", so that he cannot be blacklisted for further deputation.

And so the game of hide and seek goes on, till one day, in the right *mahurat* the name is sent to the right Ministry and is picked up. This time around, the Chief Minister has no problem in relieving the officer overnight so that he can take over before some one else queers the pitch.

It is a treat to see these go-getters in action once they have settled down. When they arrive in their offices around noon, there is a long queue of favour-seekers outside. They know whom to call in and whom to fend off, how much time each person is to be made to wait, whose invitation for dinner to accept. Their evenings are hardly ever spent at home and the neighbours are envious eyewitnesses to the streams of cars that come loaded with gifts.

There are rumours that the new economic policy has changed all this. The corridors of power are said to be empty and the waistlines of these former potentates are threatening to shrink back to normal. One would have liked to believe this as a pleasant hypothesis if one did not know the bureaucrat's obsession with power. Many of them are so fond of it that they bid good bye to high positions in the private sector in order to enter the lofty portals of the civil services.

All that the bureaucrat will permit is nomenclatural change. The Chief Controller of Import and Export might be renamed as the Director General of Foreign Trade. But that is about all.

Even in other respects there is a reluctance to shed power. At a recent party I happened to meet a senior officer posted at Air Headquarters. He told me how for years the Chiefs had pressurised the government to decentralize the integrated finance network to their headquarters. At long last, the proposal was agreed to and an Internal Financial Adviser duly reported at Air Headquarters. The first circular issued by him stated that henceforth no purchases should be made without his prior concurrence. Resultantly, now proposals for local purchase upto Rs 30,000, which were within the delegated powers of Air Headquarters so far, have also to be sent to the IFA. The officer seemed shocked at this; I told him that financial delegations often led to such contrary results.

But finance people do not always have the last laugh. The administrative Ministries have also devised their own defense mechanisms. Economy measures are a good example of this. Ever so often, government announces a 10 per cent cut in posts. All Ministries set up Committees to implement the decision. Interminable meetings are held but it is difficult, almost impossible to trim the fat anywhere. Still a manful attempt is made and a few posts are surrendered here and there. Meanwhile, however, in a silent, unobtrusive manner the Ministry has managed to obtain sanction for a massive influx of new posts. No wonder the size of the bureaucracy expands at the inexorable growth rate of 5.75 per cent as calculated by C. Northcote Parkinson.

A similar exercise in futility is the annual ritual of a 10 per cent cut in Travelling Allowance. Had it been implemented sincerely, its accumulated impact would have rendered all bureaucrats immobile. Only fools forbear from travel for want of budgetary allocation. Wise men gad about merrily, knowing that finance is a mindless ass which treats "actuals" as a normative measure of genuine need. The more you spend, the more is given unto you.

Delhi is a strange place. The corridors of power seem to reek of illogical absurdities and insoluble conundrums. Many find it too much for their nerves and resort to flight. But a fortunate few who shrewdly learn the ropes fast are able to KO the champions of yesteryear and win the crown.

Let us take first a sample failure. A post-graduate degree holder in economics from Jawahar Lal Nehru University had a successful career in his State. His last posting was as Deputy Commissioner of a peaceful district. He had a rambling mansion of a house, an army of servitors, the first position in society. Everything went like clockwork. He worked like a horse but never felt fatigued. In the evening, he went to the club, played badminton and bridge, had a couple of drinks and came home pleasantly tired, but not too tired for a romp in bed before he fell asleep.

He has been in Delhi only for a year but it seems like ages. He has not been allotted a house. His household effects rot in a friend's garage. He had to move heaven and earth to get his children admitted to a good school. He cannot afford a car, but finds that bus travel no longer yields the pleasure it did when he boarded the U Specials in his college days. Every evening he goes out with a shopping bag looking for vegetables. The prices appall him and he is often reminded of the kitchen garden that bloomed so effortlessly in his bungalow back in the district.

What he desperately wants to do is go give up Delhi for good and never come back. And if it were not for the dreaded E O he would have vanished long ago.

But wait! Let us look at this other specimen. An ambitious young man this, he has his head screwed the right way on his shoulders. His vision is clear and unclouded. He is using the service as a pedestal to his real goal—United Nations. He knows exactly how to set about it. He joins the Forest Service and spends two years in it. A further exam and he is in the IAS. He manouvres postings in the forestry sector, which is not difficult. He writes a thesis on the environment and bags a PhD. He goes on deputation to the Tata Energy Research Institute. Meanwhile, he has built contacts with the FAO and goes on short-term consultancies.

Where is this young man headed? Any nitwit can predict his career graph. In the next three years he will publish two books and eleven papers on ecology, wind energy, appropriate technology and non-conventional energy sources. He is headed straight for the FAO and no one can stop him. Not even the formidable E O.

For those in the know there are beautiful careers lying around just for the asking. Three of my friends who were posted to the nondescript desk of family planning in the Ministry of Health have since migrated to the greener pastures of the United Nations Family Planning Association.

Right here in Delhi, under our very noses, there are all kinds of positions available under the ILO, UNICEF and UNDP, with unedifying titles like Senior Technical Officer on Rural Sanitation and the like, but carrying pay packets ranging from Rs 45,000 to Rs 80,000 a month, free of Income Tax. Yes, Sir. Right here is Delhi. All you need is the talent, the qualifications … and the right relatives.

For those not so resourceful, there could be a plum posting in a Western Capital, an Eastern Capital or the capital of a less developed country. Or a short-term consultancy for two months that would yield a couple of lakhs. Or a three-month seminar at the IMF. Or a two-week symposium (with spouse) on board a luxury liner from Madras to Singapore. Or a one-week training course in a five-star hotel at Kathmandu.

Or a five-day training programme in the National Institute of Rural Development which is located in a rural waterless tract called Rajendra Nagar on the outskirts of Hyderabad. But in that case, why not just stay at home? Delhi can be as rural and waterless a tract as one could wish.

Talking of rural tracts, I am reminded of Indian style wrestling which one can truly enjoy only in the *dangals* held on festive occasions in villages. It is a treat to watch the wrestlers trying various grips and holds to force each other into the dust.

A sport one can watch with similar fervour in Delhi is an appointment to some high office. There was a time when seniority in the civil list was a definitive factor which clinched the issue, somewhat like the right of Lord Rama to the throne of Ayodhya under the law of primogeniture. This law prevailed because the Bharatas recognized it and refused to be inveigled into rulership despite the machinations of the Kaikeyis and Manthras.

By the time the Moghuls came to India, the rules of the game had been re-written. Each time an emperor kicked the bucket, all his sons preferred equally valid claims to the throne. And so there were no peaceful transitions of power, only wars of succession. It is obvious that today the Moghul example is more potent than the Ayodhya precedent. And so when a high dignitary retires, the air is rife with rumours. Holds and grips are debated with relish. Bets are laid on who the ultimate victor would be.

This is truly the city of Bumbledom!

32
Kissa Kursi Ka

Statutory Warning. The Surgeon General has determined that reading this chapter can lead to a rise in the blood pressure of members of all other services.

This is a tricky topic. Ordinarily, on world issues like the Gulf crisis or a United Europe, you will not find anyone as objective as yours truly. But let it be a question of IAS vs the Rest and the mind seems to go into tail-spin. I become highly selective in the choice of facts. This would account for the sweeping generalisations I have made without adequate proof. It would be advisable to take a tranquilliser before you venture further.

Placed as the IAS is at the highest pedestal, it is but natural that everyone else is trying to pull it down. Being there, the IAS is, not unexpectedly, wanting to stay put. Shorn of the rhetoric and in gutter dialect, it is nothing but *kissa kursi ka*.

The case against the IAS is simple. It is castigated as the last outpost of the Empire, a vestige of our colonial past, a feudal structure fit for administration of status quo but totally unsuited to the dynamics of change. It is reviled as hide-bound, reactionary, rigid, rule-ridden, regulatory, generalist, jack of all trades, anachronistic and antedeluvian. It is said to symbolize the worst traits of bureaucracy—the red tape, officiousness, authoritarianism and arbitrary exercise of power. IAS officers are seen as smug, complacent, snooty, pipe-smoking, public school products, having an urban, upper class, elitist bias. They are denounced as glorified clerks, paper pushers and ballpoint scratchers. The acronym itself is expanded in all kinds of comic configurations. Witness 'I Am Sorry', 'Indian Avatar Service', 'Invisible After Sunset' et al.

The history of the last four decades of the IAS is one of retreat. Bastion after bastion has fallen to the specialist services. If the Service survives still, it is because exclusive, organized services have not as yet emerged in certain areas. The IAS also knows how to shift ground. Vanquished in one field, it carries the war into enemy territory and attacks the soft underbelly where the foe is most vulnerable.

Time was when judicious ICS officers, instead of getting the boot, were inducted into the judiciary. Today, an even-handed IAS officer, if not cashiered, can at best hope to find a perch as Member, Board of Revenue or Director, Institute of Public Administration.

I remember having tried judicial cases in my youth and writing judgement in long hand (those days there were no stenos with SDMs). Criminals used to tremble at my name, for when I convicted a man, he got the full blast of my armoury—two horrendous years of Rigorous Imprisonment.

Then came the separation of the judiciary from the executive. If anyone terms one of the chief causes of today's chaotic situation as the fact that malefactors no longer fear their executive magistrates, he could be hauled up for contempt. So I am not saying it.

Some time back, Chief Secretaries of States were summoned to Delhi and asked to suggest certain measures to improve the law and order situation in the country. Characteristically, they suggested that the trial of certain local and special laws, for offences connected with excise, arms, traffic, gambling and the like be transferred back to the executive. Was there an uproar at this eminently reasonable suggestion? The din has not yet died down.

Of course, the idea of Administrative Tribunals has not been similarly sent to limbo but the reason is obvious. When IAS officers retire, they want to do something useful for the country till the age of 62 and so the Tribunals. Despite these patriotic sentiments, it was unfairly seen as an IAS conspiracy to grab a chunk of the judiciary's bailiwick. By the time they were done with it, there was a judge to every administrative member in a Tribunal. Now if the Tribunals do not turn out to be the speedy forums that were envisaged, the IAS would be blamed. No one will notice the death of a good idea.

Let us take a look at how the police has been trying to overthrow the IAS. In the olden, golden days even the Inspector General of Police was a position reserved for the ICS. Today, they are threatening to take over the Home Secretaryship. District Magistrates used to write the ACRs of Superintendents of Police. Many States have succumbed to the IPS lobby and made the DIGs write the report instead. What a DIG sitting in his distant Range headquarters is supposed to know about district affairs, God alone can tell. And my latest demand is that the IGP's (or DGP's) report should be inscribed by neither the Home Secretary nor even the Chief Secretary. Only the Home Minister will do. Very flattering, no doubt, to the political masters that at least *they* are being trusted with the onerous task!

The National Police Commission would have none of this. It is the politicisation of the police that has rendered it such a feeble instrument, if you please. The Commission wants the country to insulate the police from pressure. They should be allowed to do their own thing. One shudders to even imagine the consequences of such a footloose gendarmerie.

Newspapers often unwittingly provide clues to truth. Many will recall the box item saying that there was no crime in Delhi on a day when the police were on strike. I remember an old advocate telling me how there used to be no crime in the hilly areas of Kangra district till they got an SHO from Punjab Police, who invited some bootleggers over. Theoretically, at least, it is possible to wipe out crime if we abolish the police.

A similar story is said to have been repeated in metropolitan cities where the introduction of the Commissioner of Police system, which functions without magisterial control, has given rise to the *hafta*, the *matka*, the *dada*, the open auction of police stations to the highest bidder and so on.

Talking of uniformed services leads one to the defence setup, a sacred cow you are not supposed to touch. There was a time when the Defence Secretary was really the boss who called the shots. Over the years, the Chiefs have moved up in the Warrant of Precedence till they overtook the Cabinet Secretary. What this has done to the Defence Secretary's effectiveness as a coordinator need not be dilated upon. It is only a question of time before the Defence Ministry is wound up and the generals start talking directly to the ministers. And if someone cribs about the need for civil control over the armed forces, they will look you innocently in the eye and ask, "Are Ministers un-civil?".

There are the so-called technocrats, who resent the control by generalist administrators. In the process, engineers have given up their Mistership and assumed the prefix Er, not bothered that it sounds like an interjection expressing hesitation or a pause in speech. The agricultural scientists call themselves IARS, which is the closest any service has come to the IAS, apart from the audit chaps who are known as the IAAS.

An engineer is right when he says only he can build a bridge. The IAS officer's counter-argument is that the engineer cannot decide where to build the bridge, what amount should be spent on it in a particular financial year or even whether the bridge need be built at all. The agricultural scientist has discovered a new high-yielding variety and is keen to promote its use. The IAS officer wants to coordinate the entire effort of boosting agricultural production, of which the new seed will be only one element.

The whole thing boils down to this: Will there be an educated, literate, well-informed, widely experienced band of administrators to guide overall planning, policy formulation, financial allocations, coordination, management, monitoring, evaluation and so on? Or can all this be left to myriad mobs of super-specialists, who do not speak one another's language and would not understand it if spoken? Put this way, the answer stares you in the face. (That is why it has been put this way).

The field of education is a peculiar one. Every citizen of this ancient nation seems to know what is wrong with the educational system and how it should be refurbished. Educationists have not improved matters by splitting their subject into divisions and subdivisions. One of them is well-versed only in nursery education, while another has specialized in adult education of the geriatric variety. There is no one on earth who can talk about the system in holistic terms.

This is an open invitation to the generalist and no wonder the IAS has filled the breach. There are Secretaries and Directors of Higher, High, Secondary, School, Primary, Vocational, Adult, Functional, Pre-school, Value and other brands of education drawn from the IAS. But the crowning glory of the IAS achievement is the cornering of the prestigious posts of Vice-Chancellors of universities.

In Satya Yuga, a V C had to be an academician. Today he should be a Dara Singh, Machiavelli and Ayaram-Gayaram rolled in one. And if he also knows the 3 R's it is not a disqualification. Fortunately, we have many IAS officers who have had the foresight of prefixing a Dr to their names. Such people, capable of spouting academic, polysyllabic jargon, can merge quietly into the mixed crowd of VCs that we have these days. No IAS officer has yet been appointed Professor of Philosophy or Mathematics in a seat of higher learning, but it seems to be only a matter of time before we storm this ultimate citadel.

We can also be proud of the fact that the last few Comptroller and Auditor Generals of India have not been drawn from the audit service (the double-A service, remember?). Even the Chief Election Commissioner's post has fallen to the onslaught. The other posts on the hit list are Attorney General, Solicitor General and all other Generals, except the Generals in the army, of course.

What does the IAS have that other services don't? It is the *crème de la crème* of the country (Ahem!) A lakh are called but only a hundred are chosen. There is no institutionalised corruption in the service, no organized felling of forests, no 15 per cent commission on contractors' bills, no kickbacks on purchase deals, no sharing of the loot with subordinates. If an odd officer is lacking in probity, he indulges in his malfeasance on a highly individualistic basis, not as part of a gang. When an IAS officer comes to head a new department, he brings with him a breath of fresh air, free of the foul smells of prejudice and partiality. If he is cussed, he is cussed to all, without discrimination.

Above all, if he is bad you can kick him out. With technocrats and specialists, only death or superannuation doth us part.

33
Why can't you take a stand?

Often, when the shenanigans in the Government are discussed, members of the civil society ask, in puzzled tones, "Yes, that is okay. But why don't you chaps take a stand?"

To those outside the System, IAS is a well-entrenched *biradari* (community), the strongest trade union in the country. Its members cannot be dismissed due to the protection under Article 311 of the Constitution. Officers of the rank of Joint Secretary and above cannot be proceeded against without the formal permission of the competent authority. So what do we have to lose?

The worst that can happen to an IAS officer is a transfer. Is transfer such a bugbear as to convert a lion into a mouse?

I got the answer to this question while munching a toast in Administrative Training Institute, Nainital. It was a vertically integrated training programme. The young man sitting opposite was a young officer of Haryana cadre. He wore a distraught look. I probed further and out came the story.

The poor boy had been shifted six times in the last two years. Haryana is a relatively small state and the CM is in direct contact with the DCs and SDMs. This officer was a Sub Divisional Magistrate. Every time he landed in a sub-division, the CM would personally brief him about who his favourite MLAs were and to be pampered, and who his political rivals were and to be cut to size.

Any complaint and he was out. He did not have the right to state his point of view. When he tried to explain, it was made clear that no one was interested in his version.

He could hardly open his baggage before his next orders came. The children were the worst affected. He could not have them admitted to the reputed schools. No seats were reserved for the children of IAS officers. Contrarily, the CEOs of private companies had adopted the practice of making a munificent contribution to the prestigious schools. In return their wards just walked through.

To top it all, the poor boy had to suffer the satirical witticisms of his wife, insinuating that he was the only Harishchandra in the cadre.

Let us take one more example of a transfer. In the state of Tamil Nadu, each election brings the DMK and the AIDMK alternately into power. One of the first acts of an incoming CM is to transfer the incumbent Chief Secretary. I am stating all this from memory, so I may err in some minor details.

What Jayalalithaa did was to transfer the CS as Chairman, Boundary Commission. The officer's ego was hurt; in any case, he had nothing to lose as he would retire within two years. He went to the Supreme Court saying that as Chief Secretary, he held the most important post in the State. The Boundary Commission was a sinecure, with no work, no powers, nothing. The transfer was an act of vendetta by the CM. It should be set aside and he be reinstated as Chief Secretary.

The Supreme Court declined to interfere. It took a somewhat pedantic approach. The post of Chairman, Boundary Commission had been notified by the state government as being equivalent in pay, perquisites, duties and responsibilities to that of Chief Secretary. So that was that.

This landmark judgement has written finis to any possible display of independent functioning by the higher bureaucracy. Following this precedent, the courts have refused to interfere if a DGP, Law and Order was posted as DGP (Rules), or a Deputy Commissioner shunted out to the grazing ground of Officer on Special Duty, District Gazetteer Unit.

Next, we come to the myth that the IAS is an organized group of brigands, who stand together against any onslaught. Nothing is farther from the truth. The IAS is divided on the basis of caste, creed, political alignment, power groups and so on. There is lot of infighting and jockeying for power going on all the time. If the Principal Secretary to the Prime Minister is a Malayali, officers of Malayali origin or descent or those allotted to Kerala may get all the plum postings at the Centre.

Then you have the dynasty and officers who have for years been close to individual members of the dynasty. You may hear muted whispers of a posting in World Bank or IMF, followed by a stint as Cabinet Secretary, followed by Advisership in the PMO, then as interlocutor with one of our estranged tribes, finally to come to rest in gubernatorial comfort in one of our numerous Raj Bhavans.

In the state cadres, vertical schisms are not unknown, people loyal to the party currently in power and those owing allegiance to the party in opposition. Or the group led by the Chief Secretary and the one led by the Principal Secretary to Chief Minister.

Thus the scenario of a monolithic IAS pulling oars in the same direction is a myth nurtured by spectators, who have no inside knowledge of how the system works.

One last point. IAS officers are always on the prowl, looking for an opportunity. So if one officer takes a tough stand, preventing the political masters from doing something patently illegal, unethical, immoral or corrupt, there is no dearth of his colleagues who convey the message that if they are given the chance, Barkis is willin'.

34
From Seshan To Alsatian

Tirunellai Narayana Iyer Seshan has a gargantuan name that matches his over-bearing ego. He is a Tamil-speaking Brahmin from Palghat (also spelt Palakkad). With Brahmins losing their traditional vocations, they have chosen to excel in four fields—as civil servants and musicians, cooks and crooks—in Seshan's telling phrase.

Seshan had a remarkable career in the bureaucracy. He held important offices including the coveted post of Cabinet Secretary (although for a few months only). People who knew Seshan of those days summed up his character in one pithy sentence: "He growled at his subordinates and purred at his superiors". His bosses, both bureaucratic and political, thought of him as a cuddly little poodle whom one could entice a smile from, by the elementary device of scratching below his ears.

An officer who had worked with him and suffered his virulent tongue-lashing remembered his behavior as Secretary (Internal Security). "He did not conduct himself like a dignified Secretary to Government of India," the officer recalled. "He looked more like Rajiv Gandhi's Personal Security Officer, opening and closing doors for him like a portly peon."

He would have gone home but for the highly unlikely Prime Ministership of the Young Turk Chandrashekhar that lasted only three months and the Law Ministership of the maverick Subramaniam Swamy who was a personal friend.

When Seshan realized that he was now on a Constitutional post where his chair was safe for six years and that he was answerable to no one, he suddenly got transformed into an Alsatian. These days we have got habituated to organizations bearing a name with the sinister prefix El-or Al-, like Al-Qaeda. But those were early days yet.

The Al-Seshan started his career as CEC with a flourish. He forbade the reading of books and magazines by his staff in the library.

He ruled that officials placed at his disposal were, for the period of their deputation, under his administrative and disciplinary control. He could transfer them, suspend them, and do anything he liked with them.

He said that no one could disfigure a wall with election posters and slogans.

He said that he could deploy police force in a state according to his assessment of need, whether the state government asked for it or not.

He said he would monitor every little bit of expenditure incurred by candidates and deployed Commissioners of Income Tax to monitor the compliance of his instructions.

He said that no candidate could seek to influence voting by an appeal to religious or sectarian impulses.

The impact of Seshan's interventions was spectacular. Politicians were mortally afraid of him.

In distant Kinnaur, I came across Virbhadra Singh with a small caravan. "Kindly count the number of vehicles I have and report these to Mr Seshan."

During the repoll in Bihar during the election of the President, Laloo Prasad Yadav came and told me, "You can see that I am nowhere near the polling booths. I had just come to see that all the arrangements are in place. Now you will not see my face. Please tell Mr Seshan about this."

In wedding parties, everyone tried to come as close as possible to Seshan.

There is no doubt that Al-Seshan had a massive impact on the entire electoral process in India. Elections were fair, inexpensive and in accordance with norms. This was the golden period of the Election Commission.

Another notable case of transformation is that of Shri Vinod Rai, the Comptroller and Auditor General of India. Vinod was Joint Secretary (Navy) when I was Joint Secretary (Public Sector) in the Ministry of Defence. I dealt with the three defence shipyards, the Mazagon Docks, Bombay the Garden Reach Shipbuilders, Calcutta and the Goa Shipyard Ltd, Goa. Our anxiety was to get as much money as we could from Vinod, in order to give a boost to our marine warfare capability.

I remember Vinod as a bright officer with a rare equanimity. We hit it off like a house on fire.

This essentially simple Vinod who could not say "Bo" to a goose has now taken on the mighty Government of India. Vinod crosses swords with the PM almost on a daily basis.

Every two months, with a terrifying punctuality, Vinod lights a fuse and bursts a bomb under the doddering bottom of a beleaguered Manmohan Singh. What was known worldwide as the lilywhite reputation of a man who still possessed only a Maruti 800 car is today bespattered with mud. All thanks to Vinod!

What gives Vinod this indomitable courage? How did this David acquire the courage to take on single-handed all the Goliaths of the UPA government? Just one provision in the Constitution that makes the CAG's dismissal a highly difficult, an almost impossible, act. Vinod has a guaranteed stay of six years in his chair.

The simple moral of this story is that if you can insulate an authority from unwholesome pressure from the party in power, that authority will deliver.

That is why the Fifth Central Pay Commission, of which I was the Member-Secretary, recommended that minimum tenures be prescribed for certain critical posts and no premature transfer permitted unless an independent Civil Service Board examined the allegations against him and recommended a premature transfer.

In other words, for those posts, the government should have the right to appoint, but not to dis-appoint!

35
The Political Masters

Whenever a bureaucrat refers to a minister as his political master, there is a satiric glint in his eye. For the IAS racehorses can be ridden masterfully only by jockeys whose '*girip*' is '*tat*', as Nawal Singh, the legendary riding instructor of Mussourie Academy used to say. Numberless are the ministers who made a premature claim to having broken in a particularly mettlesome officer, only to bite the dust soon afterwards.

The much-maligned file, which is often dismissed as a moth-eaten relic of a colonial past, provides the arena where the battle of wits is fought. A wily bureaucrat sends up a trial balloon in the form of a note suggesting a course of action on some totally innocuous matter. The file comes back duly signed by the minister. A week later, another note is smuggled in, half-smothered in a bulky folder, now advocating a diametrically opposite line of action on the self-same issue. Will the minister meekly sign the second note? This is the acid test that determines whether he will be master or slave.

Wary ministers tend to lean on their personal staff, in order to avoid such bloomers. This leads to the Peshi system of dealing with files, which invests these minions with such terrifying power. A mechanism whose hoary antiquity is lost in the mists of time, the Peshi system assumes that the minister cannot read the file himself. Even highly educated judges have readers. Ministers, being largely unlettered, have Principal Secretaries, Special Assistants, Personal Secretaries and people with other honorific tides, but basically all are readers or *peshkars*.

The Peshi system is like an opiate, cosy, comfortable and kind to the grey cells. *The peshkar's* voice drones on, forgetting, mixing up, twisting facts, while the minister thinks of something more important or even takes a cat-nap. When the sound stops he opens his eyes, red with reflection, and asks, "So what do *you* think should be done?"

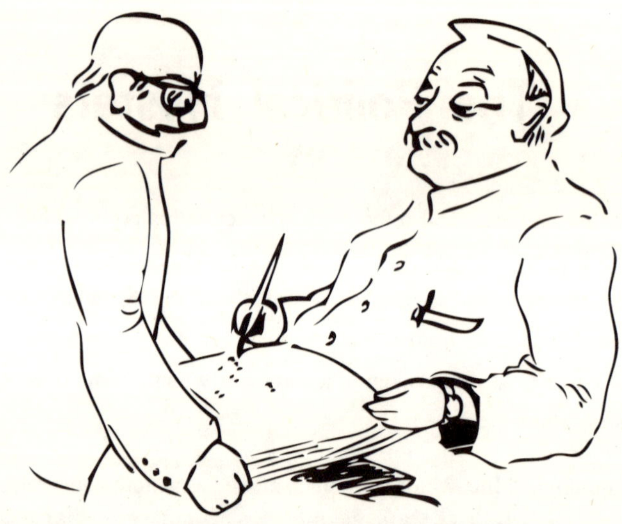

Ministers who actually read files are as rare as the dodo. The day a minister refers to para 5(a) (ii) of letter no. 1035(69) /23/89(EB) dated 20.03.90 at page 132, his reputation skyrockets to Mars. The ultimate compliment that an IAS officer can bestow on his minister is: "He reads files almost like a bureaucrat."

One of the puzzling myths of the democratic system is that ministers make policy and civil servants implement it. In practice, when long-winded theses on policy are presented to politicians they yawn and wear that special glaze on their corneas which tells the experienced observer that they are asleep with eyes open. Their sole interest is in the nuts and bolts of administration. The typical response of a minister is: *Arre bhai*, you make any import policy you wish to. I only want that Messrs X, Y and Z should get import permits ..."

Keen type bureaucrats, who boast of their primary allegiance to public interest, frame strait-jacket policies in an attempt to restrict what they consider an arbitrary exercise of discretionary power by the political bosses. These are the ubiquitous rules, so beloved of bureaucrats and so reviled by politicians.

A freshly-minted minister assumes office with a vague notion that he is an omnipotent overlord whose merest wish has to be translated into Government Order. Very soon he finds that every decision hinges on some policy, clause, rule, section, regulation, guideline, instruction, precedent or what have you. He feels hemmed in, claustrophobic and is apt to lash out at rigid, inflexible bureaucrats. The worst epithet he can fling at his secretary is that he is "rule-minded".

Astute civil servants, therefore, keep an escape route open, just in case. They oppose an unethical deviation from the norm to a reasonable degree. The moment they sense that the minister will not budge, they change their tune. Suddenly they find that the

policy does not, in fact, apply to the instant case or it is covered under the exceptions or government has powers to relax the rule in appropriate cases. This accounts for the oft-repeated jibe: "Show me the man and I'll show you the rule".

A minister does not wait for the right Secretary to turn up, so that they can hit upon a correct equation. If he is rigid, the minister travels down the ladder and patronizes the functionary who will toe the line. In these days of genetically flexible backbones, his journey is not a long one. If the Secretariat is arid, he moves into the Directorate where a rich harvest awaits him. I know of an Education Minister and a Director of Education, who between them transferred 10.000 teachers before the Secretary got wind of it.

How do tough bureaucrats survive, if they are so universally despised? The key to the mystery lies in the game of politics. A Chief Minister is forced to yield the prestigious PWD portfolio to his prime detractor: it is the wish of the High Command. How to clip his wings? The simplest solution is to post Ramrod Ramaswamy as PWD Secretary. In God's enchanted garden, even cacti and thistles have their uses.

Another area is law and order. After the politicians have finished mucking up an area and the stink has risen to Mount Olympus, everyone starts asking: How to bring about order out of chaos. That is the time to draft Toughie Talwar as the Deputy Commissioner of the disaffected district.

A minister's chief concern is his bailiwick, from where he hopes to be elected next time and every time till ever. That is his base and he can ignore it at his peril. There are any number of instances where a politician got so engrossed in the power-play at headquarters as to forget his constituency. Five years later, he had all the grandmaster moves taped out but a dark horse kicked him back to the pavilion.

No wonder then that a minister's first question from a fresh portfolio is: what can it do for Berhampur. If he is the health minister, the query answers itself and Berhampur gets an overdose of dispensaries. But if he has Civil Aviation, can he locate an airport in that back of beyond?

To the student of economics it may seem that he cannot. Surely there are pundits sitting in the Planning Commission to prevent him. Surely the Internal Rate of Return will prove an impenetrable barrier. Surely, Vayudoot experts would have done their traffic surveys and drawn up a list of priority stations. Surely, the Cabinet will not approve.

All this is true. But pliant bureaucrats can fiddle with the ERR, a resurvey might show a hitherto unsuspected potential and if he cleverly juxtaposes the proposal to another one in the PM's constituency, well …

A perceptive bureaucrat never tells his minister that Berhampur cannot have the steel plant, oil refinery or atomic power station that he has set his heart on. Ministers sometimes behave like little children and their day-dreaming has to be nurtured. No harm in ordering a resurvey that will take a couple of years. Hopefully, there would be a Cabinet reshuffle by that time.

Constituency people demand jobs, but the Ramrod Ramaswamys have set up public service commissions, recruitment boards and selection panels with vague notions of people with merit getting the jobs. How can the noble but illiterate denizens of Berhampur acquire that elusive quality called merit by these brown sahibs? No, no, no, Sir, merit will not do.

So the pressure builds up and pliant Parthasarathy who hopes for an extension in service fills all his vacancies from Berhampur. Toughie Talwar, reluctant to patronize the minister's constituents, finds himself suddenly shifted to Andaman Islands where he spends his time fruitfully, studying the matrimonial habits of a vanishing tribe.

Preparing the minister for the House is like readying a truant scholar for the Annual Examination. There are language problems. English may have to be scribed in Urdu, or Hindi in Roman script. A farsighted minister who will not use glasses may need a four-fold enlargement of the text. A brash youth may refuse a briefing and then come a cropper. An artless novice, coached for hours that he should in no case give an assurance, may begin his reply with the phrase, "Sir, I would like to *assure* the Hon'ble Members ..."

Bureaucrats sitting in the official gallery when Question Hour is on are a treat to watch. They flush pink over *a faux pas*, exult wickedly when the minister nips a supplementary in the bud and are on tenterhooks when they see him falling for a trap. It is a battle by proxy. At the end, they loyally troop into his room and mutter the ritual words of encouragement over the brilliance of his replies. Privately, they might call the whole thing a wash-out.

When officials prepare the draft reply to a debate, they do not consult official reports and documents alone. Jokebooks, compilations of couplets and even the Ramcharitmanas are standard reference material, for the minister may suddenly call for a jest, an Urdu *sher* or a *chaupayi* to embellish the text. Of course, it is not uncommon for the minister to start the joke with the punch-line or to mar the poetry with a gauche garbling of words.

The equation that a bureaucrat strikes with his minister also depends to a large extent on their respective backgrounds. An officer nurtured in Western etiquette may find his rustic minister's habit of taking his soup with a sibilant s-o-o-o-p as disgustingly uncouth. A minister not averse to a daily dose of half a bottle of choice Scotch may not exactly hit if off with a nimbupani-guzzling teetotaller of a secretary, who also treats drinking as a vice. A politician from patrician stock in a pinstripe suit may look with aversion at the sideburns of an upstart administrator whose loud check shirts make him look like a buffoon. There is the documented case of an innocuous Commissioner of a Division being labelled as arrogant merely because he kept puffing at a recalcitrant pipe in meetings.

Over the years the politicians have learnt the tricks of the trade and bureaucrats find it increasingly hard to counter their awesome power with wile and guile. Time was when a minister's raising an eyebrow at a bureaucrat was deemed sufficient punishment for a lapse. Today, the newspapers are crammed with reports of arrests, dismissals and suspensions of IAS officers. Perhaps the service has deteriorated and needs the whiplash of public chastisement. Or maybe, the IAS officer is just a convenient whipping boy.

36
Takht Or Takhta

Recently, a State went to polls. As soon as it was clear that K who had been Chief Minister a decade ago would be returning to power, people starting congratulating P, his Principal Secretary the last time around. It was readily assumed that P would be CM's choice once again. As later events proved, the surmise was not erroneous.

Twenty-five years ago, such transparent, public identification of a bureaucrat with a political party or figure was unheard of. It would be considered not the done thing, irregular, even immoral. An odd officer straying on to the prickly path of undue familiarity with politicians would be summoned by the top boss and given a rap on the knuckles. Today, it is astonishing how quickly the youngsters pick up the ground rules. I had an opportunity to meet a batch that had just gone through a grind in the districts and was back in Mussourie for the final polish. They were one in their appraisal that bureaucrats were ciphers in the new system; only politicians mattered. It took me twenty years to learn this primary truth about government and I picked it up the hard, messy way. Of course, the rules of the game have also been altered beyond recognition.

When I wanted to go to a district, I called on the Chief Secretary and casually mentioned it to him *en passant*. A week later, the orders were issued and I went meekly where I was sent. Ten years later, chaps could not go to a district unless they were okayed by an informal coterie of political bigwigs. And chaps would not go to any and every district. By now, there were "good" and "bad" districts. Today, I wonder if anyone can even aspire to be a DM till a deputation of MLAs from a district has formally called on the CM and sponsored his name. And is today's youngster finicky? You bet he is. He spends more time selecting his district than he does choosing a bride.

A close nexus is established between an individual politician and bureaucrat, very early in the game. One is a *sarpanch*, the other a BDO. Tomorrow, he will be district party chief and he the DM. Next time, a CM and a Secretary to Government. Then maybe, a Union Minister and Joint Secretary, and who knows, finally the PM and the Cabsec. The two play the power game in tandem, providing the insurance, pulling and pushing up, bolstering, building images, financing, executing coups, fighting common enemies, each supporting the other, all the way.

The old concept of a neutral bureaucracy has been interred for all time. That framework demanded a bureaucrat of the old school having no economic or political philosophy of his own, who tried to grasp the ideology of the party voted to power and translated it into workable policies, programmes and projects. Thus when a new government took over, there was no need to reshuffle the pack.

Today, a change of government is a momentous event for the bureaucracy. Suddenly, all work brakes to a halt. There is hushed silence, broken only by sounds of scurrying feet, as of nervous rats exposed to blinding light. The Principal Secretary goes to the new PM or CM and volunteers an anxiety to demit office at the soonest. The PM or CM makes a sanctimonious show of confidence in him. All Secretaries are on pins and needles. Telephones buzz. Rumour mills work overtime. Lunchrooms pore over possible lists. Bazar gossips bandy about names like bullish scrips. Journalists wag their forked tongues for scoops and exclusives. The tension builds up to a terrifying crescendo, with much biting of nails and tearing of hair, till the list is officially out.

Then for weeks on end you have the *post mortems* by expert commentators. They decide who has moved up into a prime slot and by what influence. There are sinister hints about some lobby or the other, be it liquor, oil or textile. Some are seen to have been relegated to the doghouse; they were too close to the outgoing regime and can no longer be trusted. Most transfers are for change's sake, to keep the people guessing and ensure that no one stays too long (more than six months) at the same place.

The unkindest cut is aimed at those sent back from the Centre, as if to infernal regions. Poor fellows, they had written off their parent cadres, hoping to retire from Delhi. And now, in the twilight of their lives, to have to return in disgrace, to beg for a posting from juniors, to suffer a reduced salary ... many prefer a premature exit from the service.

But how are the jobs graded as better or worse? To the uninitiated it looks as if it mattered little if one looked after welfare or weapons, health or horticulture. But the hierarchy of excellence is not accidental or indeterminate. It stems from what each post can bequeath unto you. There are positions where you go to Amsterdam and Paris; others take you to Tiruchirapally and Ballia. Here you are invited for cocktails, five-star dinners and luxury cruises by fair-skinned foreigners; elsewhere, you carry your own water bottle for fear of contamination. One job gives free booze of the choicest kind, expensive gifts, prestige and importance, moving in high circles, holidays with family at someone else's cost. Another turns you into an abstemious homebody.

And thereby hangs a tale. Generations of bureaucrats have weighed each post and ranked them in descending order of merit with a punctilious regard for exactitude. If anyone tells you otherwise, he is either a no-good *sanyasi* or a counterfeit careerist pretending to be a sinless simpleton.

So if the stakes are that high, where you can be either the second-most powerful man in the country or a toothless tiger munching sugarcane stalks in far-off Forsythganj, the bureaucrat will do anything to curry favour with those who count. He will not do anything wrong; far from it. All will be within the ambit of policy, the book of rules, the bounds of morality. On that, he will never compromise. But a policy can be deflected, a rule bent, a moral principle overlooked, if the price is right.

That is how it starts. The politician feels out the spinal chord of the bureaucrat. It is this innocuous organ that can give the most trouble. If lacking in flexibility, it makes the civil servant rigid, unbending, obdurate, stubborn—everything he should not be. An ideal bureaucrat should be soft as butter, yielding as wax, pliant, flexible, sensitive to the compulsions of his political master.

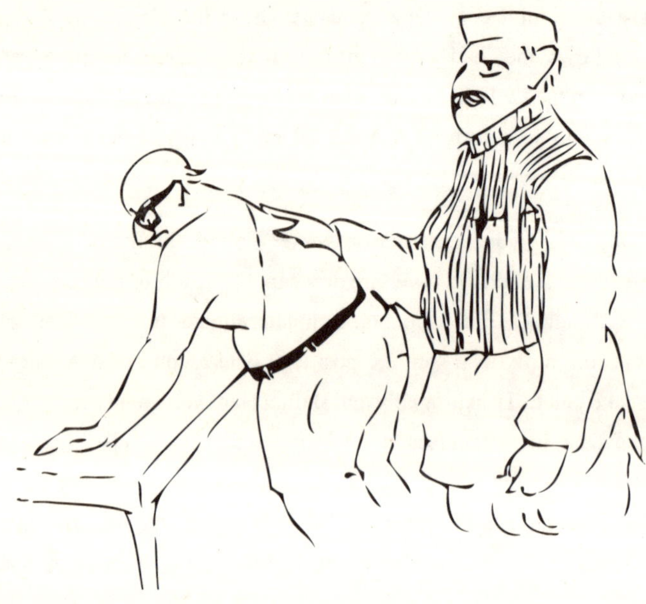

In turn, the bureaucrat tests the politician for durability. He should last out the course, be upwardly mobile, have mastered the art of survival and be astute enough to be on the side of the team that remains in saddle most of the time. He should also be a generous friend, unafraid of consequences if he picks up a Chief Secretary from the bottom of the pile, and unruffled in the face of a public outcry over the misdeeds of his favourite minion.

Experimenting as they go along, the pair progress on the thorny road to the top. The bureaucrat is converted into a member of the politician's family. He is witness to the time when the son turns into a naxalite nihilist, and helps the hapless father win him back slowly to the humdrum comfort of the conventional rat-race. He shares the agony of seeing the daughter run way with a nickel-less nitwit, and places a soothing palm on the ruffled brow of his patron. He knows of his connections with the underworld which help settle scores with enemies, the riffraff who organize the big birthday *tamashas* and kisan rallies, and the business nabobs who furnish the customary cash without tears. He is privy to all of his secrets (or rather most of them, for the politician will not trust *any one* with all), including the time when certain papers had to be substituted in official records and the occasion on which the accounts of a certain undertaking had to be doctored. The two acquire a stupendous stake in preserving camaraderie, for a break can be fatal.

If all goes well, this kind of bureaucrat may reap the harvest of his pointed partisanship even after retirement. He it is who goes as Governor of a State, to dash off a convenient report when a democratically elected Government is to be dismissed. He is our man in Moscow or Washington, who reassures these distant potentates about his master's stability, loyalty, good intentions or whatever else is in doubt at the moment. If he is too old for active service, he can be a member of the Planning Commission or Chairman of some glorified Committee, so that his basic minimum needs of bungalow, car, PA, peon, phone etc are guaranteed till the date of his demise at the premature age of eighty five.

But such cosy relationships are not for all, nor can these be counted upon. The horse you bet your life savings on may stumble and be out of the running very early in the race. You have still to survive and try to make it to the summit.

Old masters advise a 'middle of the road' approach. Politicians must be treated like fire. One should not come too close and be scorched, nor go too far away and be left out in the cold. There is an intermediate zone where one is warm and comfortable, visible so that one is on call and distant enough to run away if discretion so demands.

When a government changes, one should be quiet and immobile, hoping to be mistaken for the furniture. Any movement is likely to draw unwarranted attention. By sundry acts of genuflection and courtesy, acquiescence and non-combativeness, send signals that the backbone has the right kind of elasticity. When the big boss speaks in public, keep nodding almost imperceptibly and convey a subtle yesmanly approach to commands. Gradually, your credentials are established and the danger starts receding.

There are some bold spirits, willing to take risks. For them, there is an audacious strategy if one can pull it off. Watch an outgoing government on its last legs with eagle eyes, till the right moment arrives. That a government is about to collapse can be judged by the way every act of the top man misfires, the growing disenchantment in the media, the opening of too many fronts, the tic in the face, the repeated appearances on the telly, the public flagellation of impotent stooges and so on. Expert observers can see the multitudinous signs months ahead. At the right stage, they commit sudden *hara-kiri*, deliberately draw the manic rage towards themselves and are sent into exile. Ignorant bystanders are mystified why such an old hand at the game should have lost his wicket to such an easy ball. But this is only a strategic retreat. Three months later when the new rulers arrive, the wily virtuoso delivers his *coup de maitre*, poses to be a victim of the previous regime and seeks rehabilitation.

All this brings us to the fundamental fact of today's life that there is no coherent, cohesive service left. The IAS consists of his men, my men, the men aligned to A, B, C and X, Y, Z. There may be a few who claim to be their own men. On closer scrutiny they turn out to be denizens of a world of their own imagination.

And, therefore, whether we like it or not, the spoils system is here. Henceforth, when a regime changes, so will the holders of the top slots in the bureaucracy. As the political war rages fiercer, allegiances will become stronger and reprisals more brutal. Transfers will no longer satisfy. Cruel caucuses will demand the guillotine. Suspensions, arrests, CBI raids, forced resignations will become the daily diet of scandal-hungry tabloids and TV channels.

Once more, in the historic city of Delhi and in state capitals around the country, men will ascend either the *takht* (throne) or the *takhta* (scaffold), as in days of yore.

PART SIX
Going Into the Stratosphere

37

The Anatomy of Corruption

There are many imponderables about the phenomenon of corruption. People are not unanimous even about the basic definition of what constitutes a corrupt act. If we lived as contemporaries of Socrates, he would have challenged us to define our terms first.

It is this vagueness about what is merely inappropriate and when such inappropriateness degenerates into dishonesty, sleaze, fraud, deceit or duplicity that leads to such wide variations in the estimates of incidence of corruption.

Talk to any of my contemporaries and they will pontificate, "Oh, in our times it was not as bad as this. Hardly 5 per cent of the officers would indulge in corruption."

They forget to say that in 1947 a Secretary to Government of India used to draw Rs 3500 per month while a peon drew a measly Rs 30 p.m. The ratio was 1:100. This ratio had dropped to 1:10 by 1997 when I was asked by the government to refix all the salaries.

They forget to say that they had huge houses with vast stretches of land which were cultivated for them by a fleet of *malies* and *beldars*. *Desi ghee*, fruit, fish, venison, teetar, wine and whisky came from diverse sources as a customary tribute from the rajas and *zamindars*.

There was an army of cooks, *khansamas*, bearers, *chaprassies*, *punkah* boys and so on, who were either on official payroll or had been deployed in the sahib's kothi since time immemorial.

They forget to mention the sundry cars, jeeps, horses, boats and other modes of travel, all provided by a benign sarkar.

They forget to count the times they were the guests of honour at functions and dinners hosted by the aristocracy, both at headquarters and during their winter tours.

At the lower levels of the bureaucracy there were payments, both in cash and kind, known by various names such as *rasoom*, *baksheesh*, *chai paani* or whatever. In one state, a friend of mine could get no performance from the clerks till he had provided a rather heavy pouch containing currency notes. In the absence of a paperweight, the clerks averred, his papers would scatter around the Secretariat, buffeted by the winds of spring and autumn.

If what is customary is all right, then our definition of corruption has to fit into that paradigm. Such people count only a wad of cash taken directly as quid pro quo for favour done as a bribe.

If you take away all the so-called perquisites of office and count every round of travel by the baba log in the staff car as corruption, then obviously 90 per cent officers would be guilty of corruption.

Apart from the definitional issues, there are also wide variations in the pattern of administration as it evolves in different states of the country. In an infant state like Himachal Pradesh, where we even had princely rulers having a territory of one square kilometer, where the king was his sole employee and collected the octroi on wandering flocks of sheep, what flights of corruption could our officers indulge in with that dismal legacy of the past? They could at best fell a tree and divide the proceeds thereof with the DFO, the forest lessee and the local Minister.

Contrast the hoary traditions of rajas, nawabs and zamindars in Uttar Pradesh, who collected the revenue on behalf of the Emperor of India and kept one-fourth of all they collected as their cost of collection. Their direct descendants are the District Collectors of today who collect 10 crores a month for the Chief Minister and keep one-fourth as their cost of collection.

Jammu and Kashmir falls in an altogether different category. Right from the days of Bakshi Ghulam Mohammad, the Government of India has turned a Nelson's eye towards all those thousands of crores which travel directly from the treasury into the capacious pockets of politicians and bureaucrats. That is how they can dare show Rs 100 crores as spent on a road to Leh that was never built and Rs 10 crores year after year as the cost of repair and maintenance of the non-existent road!

The journalists are unaware of these definitional ambiguities and regional variations. For them corruption is corruption. Even the description is vague. Bofors is a scandal. 2G is a scam. The COD defines scandal as something that causes general public outrage or indignation. Its synonyms are disgrace, shame or indignity. Scam is a trick, swindle or fraud. Its synonyms are rip-off, con and dodge. Can you imagine the Rs 78 crores of Bofors causing general public outrage, while the Rs 1, 75, 000 crores of 2G is a mere trick?

38

Why India Leads the World

Analysts around the world are mystified as to why India ranks number one in the field of corruption. Research has now yielded the basic factors responsible for the phenomenon.

The primary reason is Hinduism. The God of Hindus is a commercial God. He is a veritable bania, a *gujjubhai*, always looking for what he will get out of any deal.

The God of the Jews is a tough God. He says He is a jealous God and he forbids his devotees from having any other Gods before Himself. But Krishna says in the Bhagvad Geeta that he is very easily satisfied. He has to be mollified with some gift be it *patram, pushpam, jalam or toyam*. Even something as insignificant as a leaf, flower or water can satisfy him.

Now see the ramifications of this seemingly innocuous statement. These days when a Union Cabinet Minister asks for a bribe of say one hundred thousand crore rupees, he reminds the party concerned in divine language. "Don't you think, Sir, that some patram pushpam should be offered?"

Each of our Gods is fond of something or the other. Even Ganesha, the God of wisdom, is said to be very susceptible to ladoos.

Next in the hierarchy are our saints. There is a very ancient piece of advice concerning them: "Never go empty handed to a saint." It is not considered to be the done thing. If you do not even offer a basket of fruit or a box of sweets to a person who has no desires and who has forsaken the world, how do you expect him to grant any worthwhile boons to you in turn?

Then come the matrimonial rituals. A wedding is not complete without a sumptuous dowry. I did not realize how deep rooted the malaise was till a neighbour of mine from Bihar enlightened me. This was thirty years ago. It was not enough to say that a car would be offered as dowry. The brand, style, name of manufacturer and minimum price had to be part of a written contract. You could not say that a decent wedding would be performed. The scale of decency would have to be prescribed. You would have to state that the wedding would be held at such and such hotel, with arrangements for so many thousand guests and dinner would cost a minimum of Rupees X per plate. And so on ...

When someone gets a job, the attractiveness of the same is not judged by the salary alone. What is more important is the supplementary income or *oopri aamdani*. Traditional wisdom holds that a well-paid professor in a university is no good. An inspector in the income tax department or a junior engineer in the municipal corporation would be preferable.

To cut the story short, our entire mindset is governed by the considerations of illegal or supplementary income.

There are some attractive features of supplementary income that need to be properly and deeply appreciated.

The best feature of such income is its ambiguity. No one knows what the scale of the supplementary income is. It only needs a somewhat wild imagination to conjure up scenarios of unimagined wealth. The earner just requires a glib tongue to produce the impression that he is as rich as Kubera, the God of Wealth.

Then supplementary income is not subject to tax. It does not require any elaborate tax avoidance techniques thought up by a clever chartered accountant. There is also no tax deduction at source.

Now because no tax is paid on this income, it is labelled as black money. And as black money cannot be allowed to be found on your person or in your possession, it has to be stashed away elsewhere, whether it is bank lockers in India or numbered Swiss bank accounts.

These days, Swiss bank accounts are very much in news. Earlier Switzerland used to be famous for three things—cheese, chocolate and referenda. Thanks to India, Switzerland is now also known for its bank accounts.

Why is Switzerland one of the richest countries in the world? They do not have to do anything. They have just to wait till the holder of a numbered bank account conks off without handing over the slip of paper to a successor. Because many of the holders are thieves, brigands, smugglers or heads of State, who often die in harness, much of the money is forfeited to the bank as being unclaimed.

Now there is no objection to holding of black money in numbered accounts. And it is a specialization easily acquired. I have often wondered why our big shots earn the odium of being holders of black money. Why doesn't India become a country of numbered bank accounts? Then we can be rich without being pilloried for being the richest.

I offer the advice free of consultancy fee to all our lords and masters.

39

Baggy and Diwali Shagun

Momentous events often get off to a start, like the mighty Ganges, from inconspicuous beginnings. Diwali shagun may be termed as the Gangotri of corruption.

Let us imagine the youthful officer—full of beans and ideals—as the Sub Divisional Officer in a mofussil town. He is married and has just been blessed with a daughter. His wife is the offspring of a business magnate and her earliest memories are of daddy leaving house on Diwali morning, with the backseat and dicky of the car overflowing with boxes of sweets. They are sitting in the cool verandah in wickerwork chairs.

Enter then the wicked Lala Jagat Ram, or, if you object to that name, Lala Bhagat Ram. To the jaundiced eye of the husband, Lalaji looks the archetypal, heavy-jowled villain, who sells concessional wheat in the black market instead of converting it into atta, maida and suji. He has been toying with the utopian idea of organizing a raid on his factory, but has held his hand because Lalaji seems to know all the ministers.

In the Lala's sweating palms, there is a nicely packed box of sweets. He timidly approaches the couple on the verandah, mumbles Diwali Mubarak, leaves the box on the table and runs off before it can explode in his face.

Question: How should the couple react to this elemetal situation?

Depending on the level of his maturity the man is likely to do any of the following. If a greenhorn, he will stand up and shout hoarse obscenities while frothing at the mouth, even threaten to put the Lala in handcuffs and chains. How dare he offer a bribe! If moderately seasoned, he will exchange Diwali greetings, offer the Lala a plateful of sweets and ask him in dulcet tones whether he would like a cup of tea. And if ripened on the tree, he will ask why Bhabhiji had not come, inquire about the welfare of the Lala's brats and casually mention how sweets did not keep while dry fruit did.

The woman's reaction is never abrasive. She tends to accept whatever life has to offer, be it pastries, pancakes or pizzas. And if a voluntary offer is wanting, she is not averse to making suggestions.

This is how it starts. It is no use howling, "Dash it! A box of sweets? You call that corruption?" Remember: an alcoholic starts with a tiny sip from the tankard.

Where it all ends is another story. Twenty years later, it may still be the box of sweets. Or it could be anything from a free vacation for the family in Hong Kong to cash down in a numbered account. The enticements can be broadly classed as goodies, entertainment and cash.

The influx of goodies into an officer's home can start with something quite innocuous like a personable young man with a clean-cut smile flashing his teeth at him, while he places a basket of mangoes in a corner—"From my own orchard, Sir… I was just passing by. Thought the kids might like them." The fact is that he has no orchard, he was not passing by and he hates kids. But this is a pleasing bait and only a rare fish fails to rise to it.

From such humble beginnings, one could graduate to a bottle of perfume ("My uncle just returned from France, Sir,"), a piece of Suiting ("Genuine herringbone design, Sir. Bought it for self in London. Thought you might care for it, being a man of taste."), a case of Scotch ("I know, Sir, you are used only to the best. This is so smooth it simply glides …"), and soon and so on, to a diamond necklace, a South Delhi flat or 1000 underpriced shares in a multinational giant.

The trouble with gifts such as these is that they need to be explained away. There are inconvenient rules which require every item costing so much to be declared or cleared. The competent authority's thirst for information is virtually insatiable. And if there is a CBI raid, each item suddenly acquires an exaggerated value, so the sleuth can notch up another scalp on his walking stick, that of a goonk who is foolish enough to be possessed of assets disproportionate to his known sources of income.

This sometimes leads to ironical situations. An anticipated raid for economic espionage may lead to the transfer of a complete bar into a friend's hideout. When the stars are adverse and a hostile government itching for reprisals, even a muzzle loading gun held on an expired licence can be used for prosecution under the Arms Act.

Entertainment usually starts with a harmless invitation to dinner ("the Governor has kindly agreed to come"). Liquor is served openly or concealed in cokes. Or there may be a separate room to which you are summoned under the pretext of a phone call. Next time, the dinner is at a five-star hotel and there is perhaps a separate room where blue films are being screened. The venue may shift later to a country house, where the swimming pool is filled with wine, and bunny girls masquerading as guests take you to the pool a la Christine Keeler or to the bedrooms on the first floor.

Travel is also entertainment. Someone causally mentions that the chidren are clamouring for a holiday in Goa. "No problem, Sir," says the ever officious Lala Bhagat Ram who is Baggy to his friends, "We have a company guesthouse at Panaji". And if on occasion one does not relish the idea of the family pursuing one to a beach resort, a telegram telling Baggy to arrange for room, travel, etc, etc. finds the happy traveller lodged in a private bungalow, one etcetera keeping him company and the other fixing him a long, cool drink.

The precautions: go to the country house only if you are sure of the bona fides of your host. Let there be no hidden cameras in the ceiling. At the hint of the event being video filmed, leave. As for travel, ensure that Baggy never puts your name on a company file.

The question of cash bristles with problems. Even the simple act of taking it involves choices. Should one take it over the table or under it? Should one magnanimously omit the ceremony of counting the cash or be a cad? How does one know that the whole thing is not a trap and the notes not numbered?

The views of experts vary, but there is a growing body of opinion that under-the-table dealings are now considered *passé*, the amount is taken on trust and there is no substitute for the elementary precaution of opening the door and looking up and down the corridor to see whether any suspicious characters are loitering about.

But the taking of cash is just the beginning. Where on earth does one keep it? The old and tested method was to dig a hole in the floor and then spread a carpet to hide the hole. White ants are known to have caused depredation in such hideouts. The pit in the garden is out because of the worms. One cannot have a safe concealed in the wall behind a modem painting, as this is the first place policemen are trained to look for. If the money is given to friends and relatives for safekeeping, one might as well kiss it goodbye. Swiss banks used to be secure, but this no longer seems to be so. Poe suggested an ingenious method in his case of the Purloined Letter. But real life cops are not that dumb.

There is yet one way left. Buy a painting, be it a Renoir or a Rembrandt, a Hussain or a Souza. The beauty is that there is a painting available in the market to suit any amount waiting to be converted. The snag is that even this option will not last long. The training mania that has gripped the country will see to it that art appreciation becomes the staple intellectual diet of every sleuth. Before you know it, you will find the chap with the handlebar moustache, hover, an exclamation mark writ large on the space above his head, and then exclaim, “Ha! a Boticelli, I presume …”

Like other predators, the corrupt officer attempts to use camouflage as a protective device. He tries his hardest to look honest. One of his favourite ploys is avid participation in the “What is This World Coming To” game. He talks reminiscently of the good old days when moral turpitude earned you a witheringly cold glance from your peers in the club, of the middle-aged baldy released on anticipatory bail with whom no one would play billiards so he had to shift to solitaire and later commit suicide, and how nemesis overtook an engineer when his only son was buried alive in a building he had helped construct. He poses as the sole island of integrity in an ocean of impropriety. The stories of how his timely intervention saved the government a crore, how, but for him, the overbridge would have been awarded to X and Co, the noted cheats—these are part of folklore.

Another technique, advocated by some though derided by others, is to have an enquiry instituted on flimsy grounds against oneself. The clean chit thus obtained provides an insurance cover against a second enquiry even if warranted on merits. Those who oppose this tactic say that the mere institution of any enquiry sullies the reputation for a lifetime. If he is let off, no one will say that a good man’s honour has been vindicated. People will nod sagely, smile wisely and start a whisper campaign about the probity of the enquiry officer himself.

Some persons build up a formidable reputation for honesty in all matters—a richly deserved reputation. Once in their careers, they get a break, the stakes are enormous. The kickback is enough to last three generations and no one is likely to squeal. Just that once, the man breaks his vow of poverty.

For the one caught by the 'diwali shagun' bug, the ultimate camouflage is a false persona—that of a poverty-stricken slum-dweller, clad in rags, baulking at the prospect of spending even a paisa on the broad ground that he has none to spare. If he wears Gucci shoes and Ray Ban glasses, reeks of imported after-shave and has a pencilpoint crease in his trousers, the game is up and he might as well surrender himself to the police.

Seeming rich is worse than having deep crimson lipstick smeared all over an ultra-white shirtfront.

40

Why am I not on Her Tapes?

These days, when the sole topic of conversation in the drawing rooms of all those who matter in the country is the Nira Radia tapes, I have perforce to hide my face. No one has actually thrust the question directly at me. My friends are all polite people, schooled in the art of civilized conversation. So I know that no one is likely to embarrass me by frontally posing the query.

But whether anyone says it or not, I sense this unspoken question in their eyes. I know that they must be discussing it behind my back. There must be a thousand theories to explain this inexplicable phenomenon. Some people must be asserting that I have been a has-been for a decade now and if I had clout 10 years back (which also seems doubtful), it has obviously vanished by now. Others must be declaiming for all they are worth that my importance in higher circles had always been exaggerated and they knew it all along, but nobody paid any heed to them.

The worst damage this has done is to my self-esteem. Look at the chaps who figure in the tapes, if you please. I know Prabhu Chawla since the days when he used to ride a scooter (a Lambretta, if you must know) and wait for hours in the corridor, before the Chief Minister of Himachal would condescend to see him for a few minutes. Vir Sanghvi may put on airs now but I could jog his memory to remind him of a long chat we had on the lawns of Hyderabad House, when I was Civil Aviation Secretary, and he pumped me and strung me along till I had given him all the gory details and next morning I got the Private Secretary to the Minister reporting to me all that I had divulged about the Minister to Vir Sanghvi. And this Barkha Datt was not even born then!

Mind you, if it was only the press chaps, one would not mind. But when I find my friend and IAS batchmate Nand Kishore Singh figuring in the tapes, my self-image takes a nosedive.

Imagine how they are talking to Nira Radia? I hope I did not wake you up? No, no, no … he says or she says with a throaty chuckle. They are all on first name terms with each other. They speak of previous operations that they have jointly masterminded. They manipulate people, the way a story is covered by the national media, how the council of ministers should be constituted, who should get what portfolio and so on and so forth.

Listening to them talking glibly about 1, RCR (1, Race Course Road, dummy!), SG (Sonia Gandhi, dumbo!), Kani and the rest, I am reminded of our own Kashmiri Pandit leader who was famous for receiving calls from "Soniaji" at all times of the day or night. I used to laugh at the strategy employed by him to raise himself in the eyes of his followers.

Today, I can only weep. Because the fact remains that I do not figure anywhere (not even as a footnote) in the Radia tapes.

41

Why We Need Babas to Counter Corruption!

The recent spurt in the activities of sants, swamis, babas, etc. in the war against corruption had mystified our "intellectuals" for some time. However, the Director of the newly established Indian Institute of Corruption Management, situated somewhere north of Kedarnath, has now unravelled the mystery.

The Indian mindset has, for centuries, placed renunciates at a high pedestal. Being especially addicted to insatiable greed, the Hindu psyche cannot trust anyone with pretension to desirelessness unless he has formally forsaken the world. A Mohandas Karamchand has to shed off his western attire and pump boots, and get transmuted into a half-naked fakir, before he can earn credibility as a freedom fighter. Similarly, Baba Ramdev has to show off his adeptness in yogic contortions before we listen to his exhortations against black money.

The Institute has conducted an opinion poll covering 20,000 respondents spread over 200 cities, towns and rural areas, to better appreciate the logic behind this bewildering phenomenon. 63 per cent of the respondents have disclosed that they are more likely to believe a person wearing saffron clothes than those in white khaddar. 47 per cent feel that anyone mumbling Sanskrit shlokas knows all the deeper verities of life and can be trusted. 75 per cent of the female respondents are prepared to close their eyes and doff their clothes in a sanyasi's presence under the notion that this is an essential part of some sacred ritual.

Some skeptics have raised the bogey that all the Babas seem to be rooting for the fast unto death option. They do not believe that any of them is seriously contemplating this alternative. The strategy rather appears to be to have a chain strike unto death, in which several Babas will take part. Each of them will threaten suicide by fasting, hanging, self-immolation, drowning or poisoning, but the Government will be able to deflect them from this extreme option at the last minute. Whereupon, with the Government heaving a premature breath of relief, the next Baba would enter the breach and create the next emergency.

The Government seems to have devised an effective counter strategy to defuse the crises. If the threat is grave, the Prime Minister sends three to four Cabinet ministers to the airport to persuade the Baba not to pursue his extreme option. If, as is likely, the Baba does not play ball, the Government sets up a Group of Ministers, with Pranab Mukherjee as Permanent Chairman and Kapil Sibal as Permanent Spokesperson.

What follows is a farce in four Acts, with the meetings of the joint consultative group being held at different places. The media have a field day. Both sides keep on changing their stands from forenoon to afternoon, thus creating a lot of suspense and trepidation.

The government also indulges in several sub-plots that enliven the play. Suddenly scandals erupt about the Babas' past and matters buried fathoms deep are unearthed. The government uses the master strategy perfected at the time Tarun Tejpal delivered a crushing blow to the body politic with the Tehelka sting operation. The various taxation departments, enforcement directorate, CBI, State Police, Department of Corporate Affairs, SEBI and a host of sundry government agencies swing into action and cook up cases.

Thus, Baba Ramdev does not know which way to look when sudden disclosures about his trusts with total assets of over Rs 1100 crores burst into print. Shanti Bhushan and Prashant Bhushan find that they had been given plots and flats out of some discretionary quota. Even poor Anna gets into thick soup because his admirers celebrated his birthday a few decades back and spent (hold your breath!) the princely sum of 20,000 rupees.

Learned Professors opine that there is no unifying thread in the demands of the assorted Babas and they should first put their act together before the government responds meaningfully to the developing situation. TV commentators discover that the civil society representatives are self-appointed (ideally, they should perhaps have been nominated by the government). They are both unelected and unelectable. So apparently they have no right to advise the elected representatives of 'We, The People', who hold the sacred mandate of telling us what 'We, The People' really want!

Meanwhile retired bureaucrats, military and police officers, journalists, analysts, Magsaysay Award winners, civil society activists, people generally experienced in joining Halla Bol rallies and candlelight vigils join the fray and render the show more interesting. In the bedlam that ensues it is impossible to decipher who is saying what.

When everything else fails, there is the ever-obedient Delhi Police which discovers a grave threat to security at the busy hour of midnight and wields tear gas and lathis to disperse the unruly mob of sleeping men, women and children. Baba Ramdev recreates history and compares himself to Shivaji when he escapes from the police, clad in women's attire.

Topping the cacophony we can hear Digvijay Singh warning Team Hazare that they should behave or else they would be treated exactly as Ramdev was treated. And Anna daring him to do his worst.

Even Bollywood cannot reach these Himalayan peaks of melodrama.

42
The Horse May Fly!

I bring earth-shaking news from the training course I recently did in the idyllic though ill-kempt precincts of the Tata Institute of Social Sciences, Bombay. Condemned to compulsory confinement of five working days, only eight of us turned up out of a list of thirty-five.

TISS has given us Medha Patkar and social activists of her ilk. And Vidya Rao, the course director went on piling activist upon activist in her brave attempt to penetrate the IAS citadel of smugness.

On the third day, it happened. A kurta-clad Pimple (pronounced Pimplay, so don't laugh) of YUVA sat cross-legged on a chair and waved arms excitedly about the *jhopad-pattis* of Bombay.

One thing stuck. Amnesty International had been born just because one reader had sent in a letter to the Editor of *Times*, London.

Really! Was it that simple a beginning! What was I waiting for!

For years, I have been writing essays on the IAS, lampooning myself and my friends in the service, for all that has happened to us. When I joined the service in 1964, I was proud of the three initials I had acquired after my name. Somewhere along the line the glamour vanished. The tinsel wore off and now there were headlines about CBI raids on IAS officers who hoarded gold biscuits like squirrels collect walnuts.

Was this the service I belonged to? What could be done about it? How could we fight the malaise from within?

I talked to V.S. Gopalakrishnan, my senior colleague from Maharashtra in the course. Gopal has published three books of cartoons about bureaucrats going bonkers, berserk and bananas respectively. He holds a Diploma in cartooning from USA. So, I argued, he had to be all right.

Gopal was excited. We discussed what could be done. The IAS Associations were out. Moribund institutions, you could never expect them to decide anything. At best they would appoint a sub-committee to look into the various aspects.

Why not we promote an organization ourselves, I asked? Like Amnesty International or Common Cause. Why not, said Gopal.

And so, the Bombay Declaration was born. We drafted the charter for Integrity India, that would attempt to start a debate within the bureaucracy.

The exciting news is that we have signed the charter. Here it is:

CHARTER FOR INTEGRITY INDIA

WHEREAS IT IS THE CONSIDERED APPRECIATION OF THE SIGNATORIES TO THIS CHARTER.

THAT INDIA HAS EVERYTHING IN TERMS OF RESOURCES – HUMAN, MATERIAL AND SPIRITUAL—THAT IS REQUIRED TO ACHIEVE

GREATNESS AS A NATION

THAT INDIA IS WEIGHED DOWN BECAUSE MANY OF ITS INTELLECTUALS, ADMINISTRATORS AND OPINION LEADERS DO NOT POSSESS

COMPLETE INTEGRITY

AND WHEREAS ADMINISTRATORS CAN PLAY A CATALYTIC ROLE IN A MORAL

RESURGENCE WHICH CAN RESTORE THIS VALUE TO THE FIELD OF PUBLIC

ADMINISTRATION AND THROUGH IT TO THE WHOLE OF SOCIETY.

NOW, THEREFORE, WE HEREBY RESOLVE

THAT WE SHALL SET UP AN ORGANIZATION BY

THE NAME OF INTEGRITY INDIA TO PROMOTE

THE RESTORATION OF INTEGRITY IN OUR NATIONAL LIFE IN GENERAL AND

AMONG ADMINISTRATORS IN PARTICULAR

WE SHALL—

PROMOTE SELF-EXAMINATION OF OUR MORES OF BEHAVIOUR

ENUNCIATE A CODE OF BEHAVIOUR FOR ADMINISTRATORS

PUBLICIZE THE CODE WITH THE WIDEST POSSIBLE DISSEMINATION

HONOUR THOSE WHO DEMONSTRATE A MORAL STRENGTH AND FIBRE

AND INITIATE A DEBATE THAT WOULD CLEANSE

PUBLIC ADMINISTRATION OF ITS MAJOR ILLS

SIGNED TODAY AT BOMBAY THIS SEVENTH DAY OF OCTOBER, 1993

Out of eight IAS officers undergoing the training, five signed. The rest wanted to set up a sub-committee. So we did not insist. But five out of eight is not bad. Not bad at all! It gives us a whopping percentage of 62.5.

What will the Bombay Declaration achieve, you may well ask. Will it really transform the bureaucracy? Can anything change India?

Shyamal Ghosal, one of the signatories, who is Additional Chief Secretary, Karnataka told us a story at lunch on the very first day.

There was this man condemned to death, who was asked to choose a last wish. "O King!" quoth the unfortunate fellow, "I am working on a research project, whereby

I hope to make a horse fly. Please grant me a reprieve for one year". The king acquiesced. When someone quizzed the chap about the absurd idea and the point of it, he made a very wise statement.

"Look here", he said. "One year is a long time. The king may die. I may die. Or …" he paused with a wistful look in his eyes, "for all you know … the horse may fly."

Well, folks. That's it. We have to hope that the horse will fly. That is our only hope!

43
Committed Bureaucracy

The question of a committed bureaucracy is as old as the Mahabharata. We have the two contrasting types of bureaucrats: Vidura and Bhishma. Vidura is the epitome of the bureaucrat wedded to values, *dharma* and *sathya*, while Bhishma refuses to use his enormous clout as the grandsire of the clan and intervene in the horrific episode of the disrobing of Draupadi, on the flimsy ground that he has eaten of Duryodhana's salt.

In the context of modern India and recent times, the question of commitment made headlines in the seventies, when Indira Gandhi said that the chief quality she valued in bureaucrats was their commitment. This raised a lively debate on whether the commitment was to the country, to the policies of the government in power, the person of the Prime Minister, or the individual's own set of values. When the then Congress President said that Indira is India and India is Indira, one could see which way the wind was blowing.

Today, most political bosses interpret commitment the way Indiraji did. A bureaucrat is either my man or else he is my opponent's man. Whoever is not with me is deemed to be against me. Very often, when an officer is discussed, a casual comment that he is a good officer but of no use to us finishes off the prospect of any good posting for him.

So when a new officer joins any service, the question of commitment is one he has got to face squarely. There can be several conceptual interpretations. We may take these one by one.

Commitment to money

There is a very simple commitment possible. You can be committed to the amassing of wealth. A certain percentage of officers is currently believed to be actuated by this single motive. They assess the importance of a posting by the kind of money they can make. It is believed that the very high priority given to the two Revenue Services is partly because of this factor.

We cannot say that this does not apply to the Accounts Services, as there is no wet posting in these Services. Let us recall the classic precedent of the corrupt official who was banished from the court of Emperor Akbar. When he protested that he would not draw his salary without having something to do, Akbar facetiously dismissed him by saying that he could go and count the waves in the ocean and send him a quarterly report. To his astonishment, he found a few months later that the man was minting money. He had put up an impressive notice saying the he was the Royal Principal Accountant General of the Oceanic Waves and no ship, skiff, barge, boat, dinghy, fishing vessel or marine carrier of any sort could ply without his express permission!

In some states, it is now a matter of survival whether the District Magistrate and the Superintendent of Police collect money for the Chief Minister or not. If they refuse to, they are transferred or suspended under very humiliating circumstances. In one State, one Chief Minister used Secretaries to Government as conduits for receiving bribes. So much so that when the regime changed, the Chief Secretary had to be put in jail.

Commitment to power

Some officers join the service because they want to wield power. Many of them are from affluent households, but their parents want someone in the family to taste power. Power is a great aphrodisiac. In a country like India, many things happen to you because you are in a powerful chair. Many unpleasant things that would have happened in the normal course do not happen, because of the same reason. People flock to you for various favours. You are able to accommodate friends and relatives in jobs or get them seats in educational institutions. You can trouble your opponents by creating false police cases against them. You can misuse power in a thousand ways.

Commitment to an individual

A very common interpretation of commitment is with reference to personalities. There are recorded cases of bureaucrats who got in touch with a particular politician when he had just entered politics and rose with him. When the bureaucrat was an SDM, the politician was a Samiti Chairman. Then the bureaucrat became DM and the politician an MLA. The bureaucrat became a secretary to State Government and politician became his Minister. The politician was elevated to Chief Ministership and the bureaucrat became his Principal Secretary. Very often, the politician comes to the Central Government and the bureaucrat follows him like a loyal lapdog. The politician ends up as Prime Minister and the bureaucrat is his Cabinet Secretary.

Even if there is no such lifelong partnership, there can be very fruitful short-term collaborations, either for good or for evil. Sometimes, the two are development minded and on the same wavelength. Then the department moves through a period of very high progress. Oftener, the relationship is for evil and the department is fully saturated with corruption, highhandedness and misfeasance.

Commitment to an individual has many ingredients, some of which may be described as under:

- There is no adherence to policy. Whatever the boss says is policy. If you ask for a policy document, years would be spent in hammering out something that can be done in a few months.

- Even if a policy is adopted, it is not implemented in individual cases. In the policy document itself, loopholes are kept for exercise of discretion in suitable, deserving cases and it is not difficult for the bureaucrat to make several cases both suitable and deserving.

- There is no attempt to put together the decisions taken in a number of similar cases. Each case is dealt with as if such a matter is being considered for the first time. No precedents are quoted. The whole idea of precedents being followed unless there are special features in the new cases is not acceptable.

- The bureaucrat does not exert himself to suggest a course of action. He is extremely nervous about what the views of the boss might be. He is not prepared to hazard a guess or even to ask a direct question. Many bosses consider it a merit in their subordinates if their wishes are known by the subordinates on their own, without the boss having to say anything on the subject. The entire skill of the committed bureaucrat thus lies in guessing what the boss has in mind and putting up a case accordingly.

Commitment to the policies of the government

An older version of commitment dated back to the Nehruvian era, when each bureaucrat was considered to be politically neutral. The ideal bureaucrat was supposed to study the policies of the party in power and faithfully implement those policies and programmes, without letting his personal prejudices and preferences come in between. This was the British model of the politically correct bureaucrat, who ideally would have no views of his own.

This is a model that has suffered considerable wear and tear even in the United Kingdom. In India, there is an adverse feeling about bureaucrats nurtured in the Nehruvian economic philosophy of the public sector occupying the commanding heights of the economy. Many people feel that such civil servants are unwilling or unable to adjust to the new doctrines of the liberalized economy in a globalized environment.

Things have now become somewhat simpler, because as far as policies are considered they have taken a backseat and today there is really nothing to choose as between the major political parties. The more they bicker, the more evident is it that they are all saying, more or less, the same thing.

Commitment to one's own self

Our last section deals with the best possible conceptual framework for commitment that a bureaucrat should have. In our opinion, the only commitment that a bureaucrat should have is to his own higher Self.

The goal of life is the expression of divinity already latent in man. Man is essentially a bundle of existence, consciousness and bliss, which is in a state of flux. Through an intricate process of evolution, divinity has passed through the stages of sentience, consciousness and self-awareness. Beyond man, humanity has to move towards cosmic consciousness and beyond that to Universal Consciousness. If our life style fails to expedite the process of evolution, we are doomed to another stint of existence at the gross level.

If we wish to look at reality from a slightly different perspective, we can say that our objective should be to become men and women of character. A person of character is:

- An honest person,
- A person with a sense of duties and obligations of his position, whatever it may be,
- A person who tells the truth,
- A person who gives others their due,
- A person considerate of the weak,
- A person who has principles and stands by them,
- A person not too elated by good fortune and not too depressed by bad,
- A person who is loyal, and
- A person who can be trusted.

The world of values

This brings us directly into the world of values. There have been many studies on the concept and content of values. The NCERT had one time counted 103 qualities as values, both major and minor. Recently, an all-party Parliamentary Committee of the Ministry of Human Resource Development has brought down the number to a more manageable five. These are Truth, Righteous Conduct, Love, Non-violence, and Peace.

It would be advantageous to examine what the adherence to values would mean to the daily life of a bureaucrat. I would like to summarize the implications briefly as under:

Truth

- The bureaucrat will maintain a high regard for factual accuracy. He will not twist the facts under any circumstances.
- He will give his honest opinion whenever called upon to do so.
- This does not mean that he would indulge in criticism of others whenever he finds something not perfect. He will judge people and events in relation to the norms prevalent in that organization.
- He will say what he thinks and do what he says.
- He will not be prevailed upon to deflect from the truth, whatever be the provocation or temptation.
- He will be as transparent as the rules permit. All his decisions shall be such as can stand the full glare of publicity. He should be able to give cogent reasons for whatever decisions he takes.

Righteous Conduct

- All his decisions will be in accordance with the policy enunciated by the Government.
- In case the department has no document which contains its policies, he will have one drafted and approved within three months of his joining.
- He will follow the programmes of the department, both in letter and spirit.
- He will study the precedents in any decision he takes, so that he follows the past precedents as far as possible and whenever he does not he gives sufficient reasons to justify his deviation.
- All his decisions will be in accordance with the rules and wherever he deviates from the same, he gives ample justification for the same.
- There will be no injustice at his hands. People will have ready access to him and he will spend sufficient time to understand their grievances, call for the

papers and study them and then pass suitable orders to redress the grievance. Where nothing can be done, a detailed reply will be sent to the person, giving reasons why nothing can be done.

Love

- He will maintain an open door policy and always have a welcoming attitude towards anyone who tries to meet him, be it a colleague, a client, a subordinate, be it a high or low official or a common man in the street.
- He will have equal respect for all and give equal consideration to all.
- He will treat everyone as brother and sister and his basic approach will be helpful and humane. He will always ask himself, "Is there any reason why the request should not be granted?".
- He will always remind himself that as government employees we are not the rulers but the servants of the people. Our task is always to serve the people to the best of our capacity.
- He will treat the opportunity to serve in a government department as a unique chance by which he can serve humanity and exhibit his love for the Lord's creation.

Non-violence

- He should be always full of good cheer and bonhomie.
- He should never exhibit anger, whatever might be the provocation.
- He should keep his ego in check and understand that he is not the real doer, but that events take place by their own momentum and we are privileged to serve a temporary role in their fruition. The real action is always that of the divine.
- He should not publicize his own achievements or seek undue publicity for himself.
- He should try to avoid situations of conflict with others, even if there is provocation from the other side.

- If a conflict arises, he should always be in a mood to forgive the transgressors their mistakes. His motto should be to give and forgive.

Peace

- His mind should be free of unnecessary thoughts and worries and his heart should be full of peace.
- He should always be in a spiritual relationship with the world and its inhabitants. That is, he should be without greed, without anger, without desire, without attachment, without ego, without conflict. He should be non-combative.
- He should neither be unduly elated at success nor unduly depressed by failure. He should remember that "even this shall pass."

Conclusion

To sum up, we may say that commitment should be neither to money or power nor to an individual. At the mundane level, it should be to the policies and programmes of the party in power. At the spiritual level, we should aim at living in a world of values in order to arrive at the culmination of the human experience. Our commitment should be to our higher self.

PART SEVEN

Going, Gone!

44

Henna'd Hair, Stonewashed Jeans

At 58, one is supposed to superannuate. This frontier of senescence was probably delimited in the palaeozoic days when one became a grandpa at forty and *vanaprastha* at fifty. Today, a 58-year-old with henna'd hair and stonewashed jeans looks and feels a sprightly stripling. He turns his head when a fair enchantress passes by and is game for juvenile booze sessions far into the night. In brief, he is not tired enough to be retired.

A large chunk of the terminal epoch of an officer's life is thus devoted to devising a sure-fire strategy to prolong his service to the nation. The simplest way is to wangle an extension.

This is not as effortless as it sounds. The campaign begins with the beaming of suitable signals to the top boss: "I am flexible. I am namby-pamby. I have a rubber backbone. I have *no* spinal column. I am a born HMV. I can kiss your balls. I don't exist. Only *you* do …". And much more in the same vein.

Another manoeuvre is to be seen at the *durbar* morning, noon and night. When the T.B. looks that way, one should let out all the air accumulated in the lungs and physically become as diminutive as possible, paste a sheepish look on the face and supinely snigger, "Sar, I had just come for your divine *darshan*, Sar."

Then is the time to locate the influential one who has the cochlea of the T.B., and enlist his support. This person buttonholes the T.B. and says, "Well, all this politics is okay but what have you thought about poor Mr X? He is about to retire and the wretched man has five daughters of marriageable age. You should do something for him. Do you know he has diabetes, hypertension *and* spondylitis? Not to count an aged mother of eighty three …"

But a State Government can grant extension for a mere six months and the Central Government a maximum of two years only. Shrewd people do not squander time on such chicken-feed. Their sights are set much higher.

An eminent office like that of the Governor, Ambassador, Lieutenant-Governor, Chief Vigilance Commissioner, Chief Election Commissioner, Comptroller and Auditor General and so on is not doled out to any and everyone. Myriad qualities that lesser humans do not possess have to be demonstrated. The ideal aspirant is one who has neither head nor heart. He can be trusted to do what he is told, without needless compunctions. Special care is to be taken not to exhibit hazardous proclivities towards independent thinking or compassionate behaviour.

This may not be everyone's cup of tea. Therefore, easier choices have also to be investigated.

An artifice often used by superannuating Secretaries to Government is to set up an institute just a few months before retirement. This naturally has something to do with the Ministry one is heading. The post of Chief Executive (which has no age of superannuation) is deliberately kept vacant so that it can be held as an additional charge for the nonce, and expertise gained. A fortnight before handing over, one is notified as the full-time Director for an initial period of five years. The governing body is crammed with chums and cronies, most of whom are 'sand-blind, high-gravel blind' and not a little deaf. They gloat over the prospect of printing on their letter pads the membership of this high-sounding body, with a feeling that they are somebodies still. They can be relied upon to raise hands at the right moment and extend the nomination for a further period of five years, if one has survived the ordeal that long.

A variant on the theme is to set up a research centre of your own as a registered society and become a self-ordained Founder-Director. The trick is to collect a string of names, of high dignitaries, as Chief Patron, Patron, Patron-in-Chief, etc. This lends an air of legitimacy to the organization. One or two VIPs should be of the durable godfather type, who are acceptable to every regime and always retain their celebrity status. Central Cabinet Ministers and State Chief Ministers can be invited as Chief Guests to functions and then persuaded to convert their governments into institutional members. Starting from a tiny nibble of say Rs 10,000 for the membership, one could go on to progressively larger bites of an annual grant, a one-time assistance for library building, a collaborative research or consultancy project and so on. Concurrent evaluation of government programmes by independent research bodies is a continuing craze that one could easily turn to one's profit.

Then there is the entire fecund area of social service. All one has to do is to join or set up a voluntary agency, preferably in a rural area. For those unwilling to forsake metropolitan comforts, a rustic-looking tract on the outskirts of Delhi will do. One can then take up a project of any type: be it the desultory training of unteachable adults, the wiping dry of perennially wet noses, or the setting up of non-replicable 'model' villages. International bodies go wild about non-governmental organizations in the field of rural development, and no westward flight is complete without your *khadi-clad*, voluble exponent of appropriate technology.

There are rare individuals who seem fated never to retire. Like Jeeves, they exude such overflowing sagacity through abnormally elongated medulla oblongata as to force successive governments of every hue to consult them on affairs of State. Ostensibly nonentities, they have the ear of the highest in the land and thereby wield enormous power. Now they are having breakfast with the Prime Minister, next evening you see them on the television, dissecting government policy on momentous issues; a month later, they head a new commission on economic reforms. They are the Chairmen of so many Expert Committees that there seems to be a dire need to set up an expert committe to tabulate the names and findings of all the Expert Committees that have got linked with their names. Only death relieves them of their onerous duties to the country and commonwealth.

Who are these remarkable persons? Is it the PhD from Harvard that keeps them afloat or that prophetic paper on the environment they wrote a decade before the ecological fever gripped the West? Do they draw clout from their lineage or the stint they did as Special Assistant to a national leader? Or is it that they are privy to the secrets of those in power and are propped up only to keep their mouths shut?

Nothing definite is known about these significant questions. Perhaps these would be fertile areas of research in public administration, much more useful than all those tomes on Recent-Trends-in-Something-or-the-Other.

45
The Ones Who Got Away

Somewhere along the route, a few of us have this gnawing sensation of a misplaced calling, a career out of joint. Try as hard as we might, we can no longer enjoy the "Yes, Sir, No, Sir" routine and begin to ardently wish we were elsewhere, doing something entirely different. It is not easy to forsake the comfortable cocoon of secure service, but there are some rare souls who leave.

A few have migrated to politics. One imagines them looking at the nincompoops sitting so pompously in ministerial chairs, wondering what they have that they haven't. Being close to the machinations and subterfuges of the power game, they think of it in simplistic terms and mistakenly diagnose it as easy. Some try to create cells of influence among caste and religious groups, trade unions, government employees and industrial houses. The region around one's place of birth may be earmarked as a pocket borough. Those hailing from politicking families tend to gravitate to semipolitical assignments and become personal confidants of those in power. A rare individual may combine in his unique person a backward class, a minority religion and a tribal area. There are those with glib pens, whose scribely skills are used for ghost speeches of the official variety, then the demiofficial kind, and later the purely political stuff. They may graduate to leaflets and pamphlets, and finally end up managing the party's propaganda campaign.

Bureaucrats who stray into politics are usually disasters. Honourable exceptions apart, they are so used to sitting on distant pedestals as to make even their genuflections seem patronising. They forget that bureaucrats are never as complacent as when making rules, and politicians never jauntier than when breaking them. A good civil servant is one who bows all the time but does not really bend, while a good politician bends all the time but pretends to stand erect. The long time administrator is so used to his creature comforts, he finds it well nigh impossible to rough it out on village charpoys and home-brewed arrack. And if he commits the blunder of moving away from the safe, advisory role to actually jump into the fray, the voting pattern numbs him into a state of shell-shock. He can't believe that even his own family has not voted for him.

At the other end of the spectrum, there is a documented case of an officer who left the service in order to grow roses. Having never met him, I can only visualize a tall, gangling, middleaged man, sniffing at roses like a latter-day Lord Emsworth, stopping now and then to engage in a wordy duel with his doughty headgardener Angus McAllister. What might have tilted him in favour of a floral venture could be its relative certitude. The bud of a brier rose is not known to blossom into a blush rose. Whereas any metamorphosis is possible in the irresolute, uncertain world of officialdom.

A popular destination for the fugitives is a foreign one. The slots in the international bureaucracy spawned by scores of UN organizations are available on the basis of birth (into a well connected family), domicile (in a desk of the corresponding Central ministry) and friendship. Having once got used to a standard of living measured by a tax-free monthly wage of a hundred thousand rupees, it can be a trifle inconvenient to move back to the native country and a mere six thousand. By this time, the daughter is at Cambridge and the son at Harvard, and the wife is looking forward to that holiday on the Riviera. And so, the voyager does not return.

Just to maintain balance, one would now like to mention the sole adventurer who has left in order to write poetry. A little bird tells me how bureaucratese threatened to smother the muse in him. He saw a fellow Sunday-versifier choose the title "Poem Under Consideration" (PUC), and dreaded the day when he would write "Fresh Rain" (FR). Far from feeling respect for the beaked nose of his boisterous boss, he day dreamt the living metaphor of a vulture, while seated in a conference with him. When this led him, in a fit of alliterative glee to the apocalyptic vision of a vulpine vulva, he knew that he could no longer carry on the routine business of governance and put in his papers. Now he lets the hair grow as long as it can despite his baldness and wears a coarse brown Jawahar jacket over white churidars. And in that disguise and at a distance from Caesar, he no longer dreads the fate of Cinna, the poet.

Quite a few wanderers enter the glamorous world of big business. A corpulent salary, unimagined perks and an Anglo-Indian lady secretary entice them away. Those who value money above everything else are quite content in the new milieu. Gone are the trousers with shiny seats and jackets with darned cuffs, the anxiety about the wife's hour-long STD conversations, the petty concern over the magnitude of a restaurant bill. There is an easy air of nonchalance while talking about executive class air travel, an amour with a T V star, the acquisition of a post-impressionist nude or that country house near Pune.

But there are some undoubtedly, who get more than what they had bargained for. A system where persons are more important than principles, even more than in the government. There an unruly boss was a slow, predictable calamity, from whom one could escape to a safe haven. Here it is either surrender—or one is out. Rampant corruption, much more than in the government. There one could avoid the onrushing waters by opting for a high, sinecure shelf. Here, one might be the emissary chosen to carry the cash. And, in the government, if frustrated, one could say it was all in the game; at least, there would be a public interest dangling somewhere as a carrot to the ass. But here it is just selling soap or readymade clothes. There is no way one can fool oneself about "higher" objectives.

That takes us to the stray cases who have gone away, in order to explore the nebulous regions of spirituality. One is now a Christian priest. Another is a functionary at the ashram of an avatar. An apocryphal account of the latter's conversion paints him as an egocentric Collector, loath to accept the swami's claim to avatarhood. One day, as they were passing by, his police chief expressed a desire to pay obeisance to the saint. Following him at a safe distance, the Collector was astounded to hear their entire conversation recounted effortlessly by the guru. His skepticism gone, he now lay prostrate before the holy man. And is lying prone ever since.

And what shall we say of the young man, who taught at a school and joined the service with high hopes of serving the poor and helping the needy. Three years of police repression and rank cynicism was all that he could take. He went back and, when last heard of, was still teaching in that self-same school in Madras.

Slightly different is the case of the brilliant scholar who found official work dull, tasteless and suited solely to a mediocre mind. He started spending his time on academic pursuits and is now a visiting professor in a British University. Another heretic is a noted art historian.

I have not yet spoken of those who left the service in disgust. There are many such, one notable example being of T who scaled the dizziest heights of bureaucratic power, but fell from grace till his very name became an anathema. Left to hibernate in the cool climes of a training centre, he decided that there were other things in life and went on to literature and publishing.

As is befitting, the tailpiece is reserved for the fairer sex. So many of them have forsaken us for the dearer sake of their husbands and children that the list is virtually endless. One cannot blame them, and I am not one of those carping critics who consider the money spent on their training as wasted. Their very presence in the dry precincts of the Academy made that one year tolerable to most of us. And one imagines that the Academy song might well have served as a passable lullaby for the young' uns.

46
The Expanded Acronym

If you wish to put down someone who pretends to be a mighty potentate, the easiest way is to expand his acronym in a droll manner. Thus, IBM could find itself designated as Institute for Bungling Morons. Microsoft may have to come down a peg or two if it is made to say that Most Intelligent Customers Realize Our Software Only Fools Teenagers. Indian school children make fun of NCC as National Chappal Chor and MBBS is expanded to read Miyan Biwi Bachon Samet.

No wonder the heaven-born service has not escaped the onslaught of wags and funsters. IAS has been lampooned as the "Indian Avatar Service" to right size those members of the tribe who take on airs. It becomes "Invisible After Sunset" as an appropriate description of those who try to ape the lifestyle of Wajid Ali Shah. And for the numbskulls who periodically put their foot in the mouth, the acronym translates into "I Am Sorry" as a permanent defence mechanism against violent reprisals, judicial, administrative or journalistic.

How far is the criticism justified? Do all or most IAS officers exhibit a nose-in-the-air attitude, looking down upon other human beings as lesser creatures?

The fact of the matter is that the combined onslaught of journalists, writers and other influential members of civil society, such as those untiring scribes of Letters to the Editor and those angelic bearers of the ever lit candles at India Gate or Jantar Mantar have reduced their status to that of babus and penpushers. A scholarly friend recently informed me that the pejorative expression "Babu" was derived by our colonial masters from the Bengali phrase for fish, of which their local recruits used to smell all the time.

The implied criticism that senior bureaucrats have stopped drafting policies on momentous issues and are now considered fit only to convert the staccato barks of their political masters into a Government Order couched in chaste bureaucratese is justified. This explains why a large proportion of those whom the CBI books for Tihar Jail are politicians and not bureaucrats.

Even this role of an extra the bureaucrat is now hesitant to perform. Most of them are now hiding behind the petticoat strings of the Right to Information Act, to insist that they would no longer obey the verbal orders of Ministers. They must receive written orders or else they will not issue even the humdrum G.O. Very soon the Department of Personnel will authorize the personal staff of Ministers to issue the GOs. Then the high and mighty IAS can RIP, that is, Rest in Peace.

Considering that the Indian Avatars neither rested nor allowed the demons to rest, the IAS can hardly deserve the epithet of Avatar.

What about "Invisible After Sunset"? Now that I am also a faceless member of that vast species known as the "general public", I can bear witness that the IAS officer is always invisible. If you try to catch him in the morning, he is deep in meditation or gone for a walk or taking a bath. In the period between office opening time and 11 a.m. he has not yet deigned to come to the office. From 11 a.m. onwards, he is always in a meeting. After sunset, he is neither in the office nor at home.

I would, therefore, say that the IAS officer is always invisible. Before and After Sunrise, and Before and After Sunset. He is just Invisible. Period.

Lastly, how does the statement "I Am Sorry" fit the bill?

I must say that this is the most apt expansion of the acronym "IAS". Consider the response of an average IAS Officer to a few simple questions.

Why did you not act?

I am sorry I do not have any authority; all power vests in the politicians.

Why did you issue this patently illegal order?

I am sorry I am programmed to obey all orders, legal or illegal, passed by the Minister.

Why did you not implement the order of the Supreme Court?

I am sorry I was asked by the Chief Minister.

You are hereby convicted and sent to jail.

I am sorry. I am sorry. I am sorry …

47

The Bada Babu Syndrome

We started this book with the Burra Sahib Syndrome. Over the decades, the combined onslaught of the academia, the journos and the politcos have renamed this creature Bada Babu, or in other words the Office Superintendent.

How did this transformation come about? When we were young, the entire population of the country seemed to be divided into two categories: those who had appeared in the Civil Service Examination and those who were preparing for the Civil Service Examination. In fact, it was considered *infra dig* for any youth of consequence to admit that he did not belong to either category. When the virtues of a match in a marriage negotiation were counted, it was the universal practice to say that the boy was preparing for the Exam.

The first signs of revolt came when academics started passing snide remarks against the members of the IAS. It was comic when the seminars broke for lunch that the most voluble of the IAS-baiters turned out to be the ones who had made several attempts to crack the examination and failed.

Then came a generation of people who slogged hard to take up a professional career as engineers, doctors, management graduates etc. but later found, if they joined government service, that they had to report to generalists who had made it to the IAS.

This is the time we had the joke that the brightest boys in a class became engineers, the second best became IAS officers, the third best joined politics and those who were good-for-nothing became journalists. But the engineers reported to the IAS officers, who in turn reported to the politicians, who were mortally afraid only of the journalists.

There were attempts to breach the system. Some specialists tried to make a lateral entry into the system. Manmohan Singh and Montek Singh Ahluwalia were two outstanding examples of successful specialists. But they had to compete with members of the Indian Economic Service, who were part of the Central Services.

I did not realize how deep the animosity between the two streams of economists was till we got Montek Singh who was the Secretary of Economic Affairs and notionally the Head of the Economic Service as a witness before the Fifth Central Pay Commission. Expecting him to advocate the cause of the IES in order to obtain a brighter deal for its members, we were stumped when Montek Singh pleaded for an abolition of the Economic Service.

Of course, the wheel has now turned full circle. Today a bulk of the persons who make it to the IAS are specialists. A fair number of them are IIT engineers, IIM post-graduates, even a sprinkling of doctors. Part of the reason is the slowdown in the private sector. Part of the explanation lies in the high salaries and pensions civil servants now draw. There are some who wish to change the system from within to serve the country. There may be a few who wish to make money.

Somewhere in the beginning of the twentieth century, the word babu, which was used for the clerical cadre by the British got applied by journalists to members of the bureaucracy, including the higher bureaucracy, to speak in pejorative terms about their lethargy, inaction and corruption. Gradually, it got used specifically for the IAS.

All IAS-baiters, including the politicians, journalists, academics, specialists, etc. found it handy as a term of abuse. No IAS officer could protest that he was not a babu. In any case, if there was a babudom as was claimed, the IAS officer was certainly at the top of the pyramid. Today, if the word babu is used, most people would take it to refer to IAS officers.

One of the celebrated examples of a senior politician using the word for maximum impact was Laloo Prasad Yadav, when he was Chief Minister of Bihar. When he was at the zenith of his power, he used to call for the Chief Secretary. This gentleman would almost invariably be a member of a higher caste. Before he came, Laloo would tell his friends, colleagues and hangers-on that he was going to avenge the centuries of repression the lower castes had borne for centuries. Then began the drama.

He would tell his PA to call the Bada Babu. He knew full well that this term was used for the Office Superintendent. When the man came and sat down, he was asked to stand up. Laloo had not asked him to sit down. He had to answer all his questions standing up. As Laloo helpfully explained to all his chamchas, this was how their ancestors were called by the landlords and made to stand.

One strategic advantage the IAS-baiters drew was the fudging of the distinction between the lower bureaucracy (inspectors, clerks etc.) who were 100 per cent corrupt, and the higher bureaucracy. By using the generic term 'babu' for all of them, there was an implicit assumption that the higher bureaucracy was equally culpable.

The latest situation is that you ask for data on babus from Google, it gives you information only about the IAS. In these days when Information Technology is the last word on any subject, this is the definitive verdict. The IAS is not even the Bada Babu of Laloo Yadav. He is just the Babu and nothing more.

Glossary of Indian Expressions

Aalaap: Opening notes of a raga

Aalu-chaat: Eatable based on pieces of boiled potato, curd and tamarind sauce.

Aalu-ka-paratha: A fried pancake made of flour, with potato stuffing

Achar: Indian pickle

Arre bhai: My dear Sir!

Arre! Koi hai? Hey! Someone there?

Asana: Yogic posture

Baira: Waiter

Bandgala: Buttoned up

Begum: Wife

Bhajan: Hindu hymn

Biradari: Community

Brahmahatya: Murder of a Brahmin

Burra Sahib: Big boss

Chakravyuha: Maze

Chamcha: Today

Chamchie: Female today

Chaupayi: Quatrain, especially from the Ramcharita Manas, a holy book of the Hindus

Chuprassie: Peon

Dada: Don

Dahi-bhalla: Salted pulse-cakes soaked in curd

Dand-baithak: Pushups and situps

Darshan: Sight of saintly personage, conferring benediction

Desi ghee: Pure clarified butter

Durbar: Court

Gaddi: Throne

Ghee: Clarified butter

Gusal: Bath

Hafta: Customary weekly bribe to the police

Hainji?: Sir?

Jamadar: Head-peon

Jamawar: Expensive fabric with intricate designs.

Kanji: Fermented carrot juice

Khaddar ka kurta: Upper garment made of handspun yarn

Khadi: Cloth made of handspun yarn

Khansama: Cook-cum-bearer

Khildmutgar: Household help

Kissa kursi ka: Struggle for power

Koi hai: Someone there?

Kurta: Loose upper garment

Lassi: Drink made of churned curd

Lota: Mug used for toilet

Makki ki roti: Baked maize flour pancake

Mahamantra: Highly sacred mantra

Mahurat: Auspicious time

Masala: Spice

Masalchi: Cook's helper

Matka: Illegal number game

Mem Sahib, Memsaab: Honorific for European married women in India, now used for ladies of upper classes

Mishti dohi: Bengali sweet, based on curd

Moonch-ka-sawal: A matter of prestige

Navagriha: The nine planets of Indian astrology

Papad: Crisp lentil savoury, laced with black pepper

Paploo: A game of cards

Peshkar: A reader in judicial courts. His function is to present case files to the presiding officer

Pooja: Devotional rites

Praitiloma: A denigrated form of marriage, where a girl of higher caste marries a man of lower caste.

Punkah-boy: Boy who used to activate a ceiling cloth fan by a rope

Sa'ab gusal mein hain: The master is in the bathroom

Saqi: Person who serves wine

Sarpanch: Head of local council in an Indian village

Sarson ka saag: Green vegetable made from mustard leaves

Shahtoosh: An expensive Indian shawl from pashmina wool

Sharbat: A flavoured sweet drink

Sher: A couplet from an Urdu poem

Sutra: An aphorism

Talofy: To put off

Tamasha: Bash

Tarkao: To evade a person with an excuse

Vanaprastha: Third phase in a traditional Hindu lifetime, when one was supposed to leave the household and go for meditation in the woods.

Acknowledgements

Most of these essays were written and published over the last forty years in *The Tribune*, *The Times of India* and the *Naad.*

I am thankful to my nephew, Anant Swarup for his help with the illustrations.